Prairie Lightning

Prairie Lightning

The Rise and Fall of William Drew Washburn

Kerck Kelsey

ISBN: 978-1-880654-46-0

Cover images:
Storm Season © Clint Spencer. Image from iStockphoto.com.
Caught in the Storm © James Thew. Image from iStockphoto.com.
Grunge Frame © Hello Vector. Image from iStockphoto.com.

Designed by Angela Wix
Edited by Marilyn Ziebarth

∞ The paper used in this publication meets the minimum requirements of the American National Standard for Information Sciences—Permanence for Printed Library Materials, ANSI Z39.48—1984.

Pogo Press
An Imprint of Finney Company
8075 215th Street West
Lakeville, Minnesota 55044
www.pogopress.com
www.finneyco.com

1 3 5 7 9 10 8 6 4 2
Printed in the United States of America

To Langhorne Washburn and AnnaBell Washburn—
worthy keepers of the flame.

Table of Contents

A Note to the Reader

William Drew Washburn—a meteoric Minneapolis flour miller, railroad builder, civic leader, and United States congressman and senator— left surprisingly few records to document his energetic life. Apparently, he kept neither journals nor papers, and no previous biographer has attempted to uncover his colorful but obscured story. William's career, in fact, is often confused with his older brother Cadwallader Washburn in the same midwestern city.

In order to clarify and enliven certain aspects of William's story, each chapter is introduced by a short scene of conjecture. Although these scenes are likely to have happened, they are fictional.

Because Washburn engaged in so many different arenas of activity simultaneously, a simple chronological recounting of events is confusing. To clarify his accomplishments, chapters three, four, and five focus on railroading, chapter six on his political career, chapter seven on his lifestyle, and chapter eight on less significant but concurrent activities. The chapters' dates overlap, just as did the many interests that competed for his time.

While my railroad-historian friends are versed in the kaleidoscope of changing names and short-hand company initials that marked early railroading's frequent mergers and bankruptcies, these company genealogies are also confusing for general readers. Accordingly, I have identified most railroads by the nicknames used during Washburn's time.

Thus, the company chartered as the Minnesota and Pacific, first built west of St. Paul as the St. Paul and Pacific Railroad, renamed the St. Paul, Minneapolis and Manitoba by James J. Hill, and eventually absorbed into Hill's Great Northern—is simply called the "Manitoba." The St. Paul, Minneapolis and Omaha is the "Omaha," and the Chicago, Milwaukee and St. Paul is the "Milwaukee Road." The Minneapolis, St. Paul and Sault Ste. Marie Railroad is the "Soo Line."

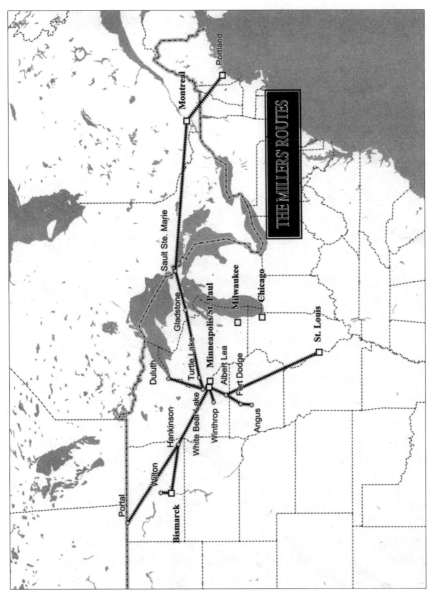

Minneapolis flour millers had need for railroads to ship their products during the late 19th century. The above map identifies the geographic locations they were most interested in and those mentioned throughout this book.

Introduction

William Drew Washburn grew up as the youngest brother in one of the most remarkable generation of siblings produced in any American family. His older brothers provided role models for entrepreneurial and political activity from the pine woods of Maine to the gold fields of California. Driven by the moral imperative to curb the spread of slavery—as well as Southern political power—they helped create the national Republican Party. When the South seceded from the Union, Washburn brothers in five states responded by raising troops, rooting out corruption, and shedding blood amid shot and shell. After the war, four of them played major roles in an economic revolution in waterpower, railroading, and flour milling on the northwestern frontier.

William D. Washburn's most productive years followed his older brothers' by almost two decades. His dreams were more concrete than theirs. Like most entrepreneurs of his day, he focused on material accomplishment more than on lofty ideals. His enthusiasms and furious energy meshed with a nation that had moved from a fight for survival to a devil-take-the-hindmost race for economic expansion.

Oddly, William's story and accomplishments have been obscured by time. He left no memoir. Published histories offer few facts about him, and the stories that have survived are often critical. In his town of birth, Livermore, Maine, and the city of his most significant accomplishments, Minneapolis, Minnesota, many of his contemporaries thought of him as a larger-than-life figure who was also arrogant, careless, and unable to take suggestions. He seemed blithe when he should have been cautious. So why write about William Drew Washburn?

Through years of research on this large family—of which, I must add, I am a member—the youngest son has drawn my attention like a moth to a flame. The mad dash of his life careens between triumph and catastrophe. He ignores obstacles. Swallowed up in a defeat, he bursts again and again on the scene with a new enthusiasm. He is by far the most exciting of his siblings.

Clearly he was a man of contradictions. Disliked by many, Washburn was elected nevertheless to multiple terms in the U.S. Congress. Imperious and insensitive, he helped found a church where he worshipped for more than 60 years. He was chosen to lead his national denomination for two years. Though difficult to work with, he persuaded investors and bankers across two continents to follow him into dozens of new enterprises. Careless and disorganized, he marshaled armies of laborers to build dams, canals, railroads, buildings, and coal mines across the Upper Midwest. Forward looking, he was a staunch defender of the status quo in politics. In an uproarious household, he remained married for more than 50 years and raised a successful brood of children. Although an important leader in his time, few know him today in the city he helped build.

Of all the contradictions in Washburn's life, the greatest one came at the end of it. He was 76 when his glittering fortunes suffered a sudden reverse. Almost immediately he dropped out of sight, his mad career suddenly obscured. Removing himself from Minneapolis, Washburn made no excuses. He returned to the city he had helped build—to the great domestic castle that was no longer his—where he died quietly at age 81. Newspapers briefly noted his passing. It was as if he had never lived there.

William Washburn's story is ripe for telling. Raised on a hard-scrabble farm in remote western Maine, he was at the center of Minneapolis's transition from muddy settlement to industrial giant. A businessman who first helped harness the power of the Mississippi River, he defied a host of "foreign" operators and, by his own energy and persuasive powers, built an independent network of railroads that connected grain mills with grain farmers as far away as the Rocky Mountains and then with flour customers around the world. His 12 years in Congress involved epic struggles with irreverent Irishmen, Norwegian farmers, Boston Brahmins, and Chicago grain speculators alike. He helped create the biggest flour milling company in the world and was at the heart of its shipwreck—one of the biggest business shocks ever in the history of Minneapolis. He helped build the city, from its street lights and rapid transit system to many of its largest buildings. At age 71, he built an entire new industry on an empty North Dakota plain. Along the way he survived bank crashes, locust invasions, mill fires, train wrecks, and fiery steamboat races on Lake Minnetonka. His story includes the animosity of James J. Hill, the thanks of Tsar Nicholas in St. Petersburg, intrigues in the emperor's court in China, and hosts of canny bankers, who he enriched in Montreal and outraged in London.

William had a full share of his family's intelligence and faith, plus his own gentility and confidence. While contemporaries resented his patrician demeanor, they remained unaware of his humble beginnings. His breathtaking nerve and ride to the top came at breakneck speed. He experienced spectacular highs and dismal lows. Of the many enterprises that he directed, he was unwillingly removed from active management of at least seven, and he went broke twice. Though he served three terms in the House of Representatives and one in the Senate, he defied both his party and his president. When he died, his estate was virtually without assets.

It is a story that I couldn't resist.

Early photographs convey a sense of nineteenth-century America as a somber place. Streets and buildings look raw, people look rumpled and uncomfortable. Furniture, drapes, and rugs look heavy and dark. People seem frozen in time and custom. But looking back this way is deceiving.

The nineteenth century was a time of great issues and conflicts for the new country. Americans had to decide whether they would be one country or several, a question they spent more than five decades deciding through the agency of a half dozen political parties and several wars. Americans' sacrifices in the Civil War exceeded all the nation's sacrifices in all the wars fought in the next 150 years.

Throughout the nineteenth century, ideals including freedom, equality, and sacrifice conflicted with the realities of slavery, prejudice, power politics, and the need for social order. At the same time, industrialization brought technological change, economic opportunity, and new pressures. The country experienced revolutions in manufacturing, communications, and transportation that changed the entire economy. New opportunities in the West lured waves of migration and immigration and still more changes to society and culture. Moral strictures on matters from alcohol to abolition pulled at Americans. By the time the century was done, they had transformed their world from top to bottom.

While the Washburn farm in Livermore, Maine, may have seemed far removed from the great issues roiling the country, its occupants were fully informed about the world beyond their fences. The father, Israel Washburn, Sr., was a leader in the community. Animated discussions embroiled the family dinner table. Over the years that ten Washburn children grew up there, they became well familiar with all the great issues of the day—economic, political, and spiritual.

The Washburns heard about the evils of slavery at the Universalist Church they built next to their farm. In 1820, in what had become known as the Missouri Compromise, Maine got its statehood through an unsavory deal that most Mainers regarded as a sell-out to slaveholders. In 1842, the Webster-Ashburton Treaty forced Maine to give up hundreds of square miles of its territory to Great Britain. Later, in 1846, the oldest Washburn son, Israel, Jr., a self-educated lawyer, won a court case that established the people's right to use the state's waterways. This began a political career that brought him to the U.S. Congress in 1850. The fight to keep slavery out of the territories carried his brothers Elihu B. and Cadwallader C. into Congress with him—from the western states of Illinois and Wisconsin, respectively. There the brothers helped engineer the birth of the Republican Party. Now scattered from Maine to California, the siblings helped win the White House for Abraham Lincoln in 1860.

Opportunities off the family farm pulled every Washburn to seek fortune elsewhere. Israel, Jr., found his future in Bangor, Augusta, and Portland, Maine. His younger siblings—including his three sisters—lived most of their lives in the West. They were smart and most of them successful. The older ones sent money home to take care of parents and younger siblings.

None received more attention than the youngest brother, William Drew. With the example and tutelage of his older brothers, and the additional advantage of formal education, he would become the most urbane of them all. Yet it was on the northwest frontier where he chose to make his career, not in the already established East. The frontier offered a lot more elbow room for a man who loved to start things and go fast.

William's story is one of many starts and huge enthusiasms. They blew across the prairies like a summer thunderstorm—full of thunder, the flash of lightning, the roar of wind, the rush of rain or hail, and then soon gone, leaving only the clear air to mark its passage. His story embodies the Gilded Age in America, a time when there seemed to be no limit to the wilderness that could be conquered, the resources that could be exploited, or the rewards that could be realized.

1

The Making of "Young Rapid"
1831–1857

It had been a long night on the Maine hilltop. The January wind howled around the farmhouse. Long after dark, blowing eddies of snow obscured the flicker of lamp lights in the bedroom windows.

"Looks like you've done it again, Patty," observed Doc Bradford, wiping his hands on a threadbare towel. "Another boy. He looks like he's all there and healthy, too. This one can take poor Will's place."

To weary Martha Washburn, or "Patty", this was good news—another son, her eighth, and healthy, too. Nothing would replace the loss of her seventh, but she would offer this one the same love and moral direction she had given her others. To be sure, there would still be no financial security, but with the money that the oldest boys were beginning to send home, there would be no starvation either. No more need for help from Maine in-laws or family in Massachusetts. No more sheriffs' auctions, humiliations in front of the neighbors, or old debts to work off.

She and her husband Israel agreed. They would name this boy after his departed brother. He would be their second William Drew Washburn.

Neither of them would live long enough to count the times this Washburn would rise, and fall, and rise again.

It seemed that the Washburn place had always teemed with children. Each year from 1813 (when Israel, Jr., was born) to 1833 (when last daughter Caroline was born) , as father Israel sweated on his rocky acres to grow hay for his animals and food for his family, there seemed to be more mouths to feed around their table and more growing bodies to clothe. On Sunday the family seemed to take up more space in the church pews. Every winter, when the neighborhood school opened, it seemed as if half the benches were taken up with Washburns. When an older one left, the place filled with a new one. Teachers who stayed more than one year recognized the handed-down clothing.

There were enough years between the oldest and youngest Washburns to insure awe toward the oldest and benevolent amusement toward the youngest. By 1831, when the second William Drew Washburn was born, his oldest brother, Israel, Jr., was 18 years old and already in Bangor studying for the law. The next oldest, Algernon Sidney, or Sid (b. 1814), was working at a store in nearby Hallowell. Both sent remittances home. The next oldest, 14-year-old Elihu B. (b. 1816), was also helping— he had just finished a brutal summer working off a debt his father owed to a neighbor and he was looking forward to a possible career in the printing trade. With young Cadwallader C. (b. 1818), there were seven children crowded around the dinner table.

By the time William was walking, there were still seven around the table. Elihu had gone off to Hallowell, but Patty's eleventh and final child, Caroline, or "Carrie," had arrived. Fortunately for everyone, William's big sister Martha (b. 1820) was old enough—and fast enough—to help raise him. Young William's siblings continued to leave the farm and late in his life he remembered only two brothers, Charles A. (b. 1822) and Samuel B. (b. 1824), and sister Mary (b. 1825) being on the farm with him.

From an early age, William seemed in a hurry. Whether it was putting the cow out to pasture, feeding the pig, mucking out stalls, splitting wood for the kitchen, cutting hay, picking apples, digging potatoes, or mending harnesses, he did his chores at a run and especially loved building things. He was precocious and furiously energetic. He was also easily bored. As he raced around the farm, his brothers, who gave each other nicknames, called him "Young Rapid."

Mother Patty later recalled that her children "lifted each other up," but none was probably helped as much as the youngest son. He grew to be the tallest—six feet—and the best looking. He was as smart as any and a fountain of new ideas, with plenty of energy to get them started. His siblings, rather than being jealous, made sure that he received everything that they had missed. After visiting the farm, they reported on his adventures to their brothers and sisters. Delighted by his spirit, they sent

7

money home so he could go away to school and wear the proper clothing. Concerned that he become well read and express himself like a gentleman, they financed several years at private schools in nearby South Paris and Farmington and, when he turned 19, a smooth transition to Bowdoin College in Brunswick, Maine.

In addition to facilitating William's education, his brothers introduced him to the world of politics. Brother Israel, now elected to Congress, found him summer employment in Washington, D.C., as a clerk in the Treasury Department. There he saw the workings of the government and even served as a clerk in Congress, where Israel and Elihu were Whig Party representatives from Maine and Illinois. In 1854 brother Cadwallader also entered Congress, elected as a Republican from Wisconsin. The older brothers found William a cot in the rooms they shared near the Capitol, and he was fascinated to watch the parade of supplicants and colleagues eager to tap into the growing alliance between eastern and western states that the Washburns represented. William saw the tumult that followed the Kansas-Nebraska Act fight over slavery that year and the subsequent death of the Whig Party. He was an eager participant as the Republican Party took shape in its place.

Back at Bowdoin, William enjoyed books and was an enthusiastic member of the Athenaean Society, a literary and debating group. As a young man, he did not drink but enjoyed an occasional cigar. He graduated near the top of his class of 58 students in 1854. Intent on following his brothers' careers, he studied law for 18 months at Israel's office in Orono, Maine, and through Israel's connections spent another six months in Bangor with Judge John A. Peters, soon to be Maine's chief justice. William was admitted to the bar there in 1857 while, at the same time, enjoying the town's social whirl. Now his credentials were as good as he and his siblings could make them. The Washburn crown prince was ready to conquer the world.

Like many large families, the birth order of the Washburn children appeared to shape their relationships throughout their lives. The oldest five—Israel, Sid, Elihu, Cad, and Martha—were always close, in part because of the extreme economic hardships suffered after their father's bankruptcy in 1828. Driven by memories of hardships, they were acutely aware of how much catching up with the outside world they had to do, not just financially, but educationally and socially as well. Dreamy brother Charles and quiet brother Sam marked a space between the older and younger groups. Lacking the intensity of the older siblings, Charles attended college but had trouble sticking with things, wandering to California where he became an intemperate newspaper editor and rabid booster of the Republican Party. Sam, disinclined to schooling, went to sea and found a career in the merchant marine trade. Both concluded their lives under their brothers' support and protection.

The younger children, including William, grew up protected by their older siblings. Mary died first—and her practically-minded husband, Gustavus Buffum, quickly married again. When Sid followed her in death, his orphaned sons were carefully supervised by Israel. Next, when Cadwallader died, his bequests continued to protect the other siblings and their children.

Young Rapid, however, moved too far and too fast to be protected by anyone. His brothers polished and launched him, but William would have 30 years of adventures beyond their protection. As the eager young man packed his bag to leave Maine, he knew that his years of preparation were over. He was now on his own.

2

Whirlwind at the Falls
1857–1879

The sway-backed paddle wheeler slowly thrashed its way up the river. On each side, steep green hills pushed up from the muddy riverbanks. Except for an occasional settlement at water's edge and some traffic on the river, the only visible activity came from hawks and turkey buzzards carving lazy circles over the bluffs.

Occasionally the great river widened. Then faster boats pulled by, smokestacks belching smoke and fire, railings close enough for passengers to exchange greetings.

At the most forward-facing rail on this steamboat's passenger deck, above the cargo piled on the bow, leaned a dapper-looking young man. At first glance, from his carefully cut clothing to the raffish cigar held casually in one hand, the young man looked the part of an indolent dandy. But closer to, there was a tautness in the slim figure, like a racer at the starting line. The casual pose belied the enormous energy behind the sculpted features. Only the eyes gave a hint of the excitement and eagerness that drove him.

William Drew Washburn had been travelling for more than three weeks. On a succession of trains from Maine, he had made a series of overnight stops in Boston, New York, and Washington, D.C. Then came the long, long train ride west across Pennsylvania, Ohio, and Indiana. Barely pausing in the thriving young city of Chicago, he charged on across Illinois, until at last he was brought up by the great river—the key to the opportunities he knew waited for him in the northwest.

William could have stayed in the East. He had two successful brothers there: Israel was in politics and the law, and Sidney was in the mercantile trade and now a banker. William's credentials were more than adequate for acceptance in the social world of any eastern city. But this young man in a hurry hadn't the patience to work his way up some corporate ladder. He preferred the opportunities in what was known as the northwest (now, the Upper Midwest). He had cousins and Maine neighbors who had gone there and were doing well. He had no doubt that he could do well, too. And he loved the prospect of an entire spectrum of opportunity—a road with many branchings. Maybe he would try all of them. When his Maine friend George Brackett announced he was going to Minneapolis, William immediately signed up to join him. The two would be friends and associates there for the next 60 years.

The northwest was where four older brothers had gone to seek their fortunes and two older sisters to follow their husbands. All had found new lives up and down the Upper Mississippi River, and all—one way or another—had made successful livings from it.

These emigrants from New England were developers, not pioneers. No wagon trains, log cabins, trap lines, or field work for them. Riding in a second wave of settlement, they took similar chances as the first wave, hoped and worked just as hard, and survived equal catastrophes. They lost children and spouses, experienced natural disasters, and got buried in debt and bankruptcy. But they taught themselves professions, carefully tended relations with financial backers back east, and ran for public office. They loved people and politics. They were comfortable wearing starched shirts and standing on a podium. Their visions were big ones beyond mere survival. They were leaders in the wave of economic adventurers that would build cities and fill up the empty spaces between them. Like their predecessors, they shared the conviction that they would overcome every obstacle and triumph over whatever life threw at them.

On their way up the Mississippi River, William Washburn and his friend separated for a time. Brackett continued directly to the settlement at Minneapolis, where he started working as a butcher's assistant. William briefly stopped off at Galena, Illinois, just up the Fever River from where it joined the Mississippi. At least seven of the migrating Washburn siblings would pass through this town on their way west, and four had already settled in the area.

Galena, Illinois, halfway between St. Louis and Fort Snelling, was the busiest commercial center west of Chicago. Seven Washburn siblings stopped there in their migration westward.

In the late 1850s Galena—halfway between St. Louis and Fort Snelling, each four hundred miles away—was the busiest town between Chicago and San Francisco. It sprawled along the muddy river bank with arriving and departing steamboats busily loading and unloading amid clouds of steam and hooting whistles. Unpaved streets were crowded with heavy wagons carrying lead "pigs" from nearby mines and primitive smelters outside of town. Herds of cattle mixed with farm wagons bearing produce; draymen, stevedores, sailors, farmers, and a few Winnebago Indians threaded their way along the waterfront. Back from the raucous scene, a steep hillside provided a literal stairway to respectability. Above the levee, the ground rose to Main Street, where mercantile establishments, banks, boarding houses, and hotels including the elaborate DeSoto House clustered together. Above them, respectable Bench Street traversed the hillside, lined with brick houses, churches, lawyers' offices, and an imposing county court house. At the top was High Street, where the strongest-legged residents lived and where their children went to school.

Minneapolis in 1857 was hardly a beauty spot, but its scattered buildings and muddy streets reverberated with the optimism of entrepreneurial adventure.

Across the short river bridge spread the town's newest residential area, where William's brother Elihu had built an impressive home that reflected his success as an attorney and now as a three-term congressman for the First District in Illinois. A few houses away lived his oldest sister Martha, married to a well-known businessman and steamboat captain, Charles Stephenson. An easy day's ride over the hill north into Wisconsin, brother Cadwallader had had tremendous success as a land agent and lumberman in Mineral Point. It was Cad's success, in particular, that had inspired (and probably paid for) William's journey west. Cad had a scheme to develop waterpower far up the river in Minnesota, at the great Falls of St. Anthony which would provide the younger man a jumpstart in Minnesota, not even yet a state.

After visiting his siblings and their families, William journeyed on to new riverside settlement of Minneapolis, on the west side of the Falls of St. Anthony just beyond the territorial capital at St. Paul. The place had less than a thousand residents. They had no idea what was in store for them.

Twenty-six-year-old William Washburn made a splash almost from the first day he arrived. Confident, well-spoken, always impeccably dressed, this Washburn had a college education, experience clerking in

Congress, and membership in the bar. In addition, Young Rapid had lost none of his notable energy.

He immediately warmed to the bustle of the place. Thanks to the happy circumstance of being located by the only waterfalls on the Mississippi River and being downstream from rich timberlands, new enterprises were popping up on both sides of the river, and land values were booming. Unlike many frontier settlements that formed around a crossroads or a steamboat landing, Minneapolis seemed destined from the beginning to be a manufacturing center. With ready waterpower, the visions that drove this place were urban from the start. Before too long the town would develop big shoulders to match its archrival, Chicago.

William's brother Cadwallader had already invested in one of the biggest enterprises on the advice of cousin Dorilus Morrison, the son of his mother's sister. Morrison, part of a group of Mainers who had been following the pineries westward from their home state, had built a sawmill on the east side of the Falls of St. Anthony. By 1854 he was floating logs down to it from pine forests he owned upstream. At the falls itself, the biggest river in the United States dropped about 16 feet, and the drop was more than 70 feet within the bounds of the west bank property that Cadwallader and nine other investors, including Morrison, hoped to acquire. In 1856 they obtained from the Minnesota territorial legislature a perpetual corporate charter for the waterpower rights on the west side of the falls, together with 85 acres of land. (Later engineers estimated that even in the dead of winter there were never less than 3,000 cubic feet of water per second pouring by the site—the equivalent of about 10,000 horsepower.)

The 10 entrepreneurs correctly guessed that a reliable power source of this size would be attractive to all sorts of businesses. Naming their enterprise the Minneapolis Mill Company, they immediately started work on a dam to back up the water and a canal to channel it to future mill sites. People started to take notice.

William hung out his shingle. From the beginning, as his older brothers had done in Maine, Illinois, and Wisconsin, he specialized in services for absentee investors. The northwestern frontier was a leading choice for eastern investment money, and a trustworthy agent-in-place could make a good living by providing services for them. William advertised himself as an attorney, a bill collector, and an agent "to invest and loan money, enter and locate land, pay taxes, examine titles, and attend promptly to all business entrusted to him."[1]

Over the next two years, he became knowledgeable about real estate law and accumulated a coterie of friends and contacts among the town's entrepreneurs. Many of them hailed from Maine. He took a room over the local bank in the St. Dennis Hotel, where he helped organize a congenial group of New Englanders. They called themselves the Passadumkeag Club. Many of the city's new leaders would emerge from this group, including his friend George Brackett, Rufus Baldwin, and Cyrus Aldrich. As William began to gamble on timberlands with an eye toward becoming a lumber entrepreneur, he would balance his business risk-taking with the comfort and companionship of a social establishment—even if he had to build it himself.

While Cadwallader's ambitious dam and canal-building project offered great potential, the Wisconsin congressman and lumber tycoon had little time to attend to the undertaking himself. Lumber prices had fallen drastically, his finances were extremely tight, and his energies were taken up fending off creditors and raising new money. As the congressman from western Wisconsin, Cadwallader was in Washington, D.C., for half of the year, joining other northern Republicans in fending off the schemes and threats of southerners desperate to retain power in the central government. Otherwise, Cadwallader needed to be in Madison, Wisconsin, wooing support in the legislature for the seat in the U.S. Senate that would open up in 1860. The dam and canal franchise that he and his partners owned at the Falls of St. Anthony had enormous potential, but Cadwallader could not be there to push it forward himself. Although his former Livermore neighbor, Otis Pray, was doing a good job with the dam construction, Cad needed someone that he could trust to spread his vision and attract new business tenants.

What a vision! Beyond the muddy streets and ramshackle construction, Cadwallader saw the roaring waters tamed by the dam, channeled down his canal, and directed into his wheel pits to drive the

---

1   *Falls Evening News*, September 28, 1857.

engines, millstones, and looms of a future great manufacturing center. To the west, he saw the finest wheat-growing land in the world stretching to the horizon. And from the east, he saw railroads bringing new farmers to raise the wheat. He saw the rails extending westward all the way to Montana, bringing the wheat to Minneapolis that he would mill into flour to make the bread to feed the world.

Cadwallader considered his youngest brother.

Thirteen years older than William, Cad was more serious and reserved—not only because of his business worries, but because of his fractured personal life. His wife, the daughter of a prominent New York City family, had suffered a mental collapse and been institutionalized, forcing him to send his two baby daughters back to Maine to be raised by his parents. Thereafter, Cadwallader's businesses remained at the center of his life. Cad dressed plainly and had an intense, penetrating gaze. He didn't laugh much, and he didn't take vacations. Impatient with incompetence, bombast, and dishonesty, he spoke bluntly, without flourish, in the words of a man who had educated himself. He made decisions for the long term and with the caution of a man well aware of the risks. Capable of great vision and an efficient leader, he focused comfortably on the practical challenges of turning his vision into reality. A forceful person, he inspired both loyalty and innovation among his employees.

William, slender and two inches taller than Cad, took great care in his personal appearance—and his well-tended mutton chop whiskers. He spoke gracefully in words that reflected his classical education. Although neither he nor Cadwallader were at ease in a crowd, William made friends easily, socialized widely, and cared about his status in the community.

William seemed a good bet to spearhead Cadwallader's vision for the Falls of St. Anthony. To begin with, William was already located where the critical work had to be carried out. He could make personal calls on potential waterpower users. He had the best formal credentials and appearance of anyone in the family. He was honest and not afraid of hard work, and he was already acquainted with many of the community's leaders.

In addition, William was about to woo and win the belle of Bangor, Maine. Elizabeth Muzzy, one of three daughters of industrialist Franklin Muzzy, had first met William in Bangor, and she later confessed in her

Washburn Library, Livermore, Maine
A young William D. Washburn, about 1860

Library of Congress, Brady-Handy Collection
William's older brother Cadwallader C. Washburn, about 1866

diary that she had never seen anyone "so perfectly stunning."[2] Despite her protected upbringing, Lizzie Muzzy was just as excited by the prospects of adventure on the northwestern frontier as William.

Soon Cadwallader made his decision. He offered young William the position of agent for the Minneapolis Mill Company. Cad would try to

2   Mary Washburn Baldwin (daughter), "Early Memories of Elizabeth Muzzy Washburn," undated manuscript, 37, Washburn Library, Livermore, Maine.

keep the money coming, and William, though he lacked any experience in dam construction, would get the west-side dam completed, see the water canal through its first stages, and find milling and manufacturing tenants for both.

It turned out to be a perfect assignment for Young Rapid. A natural, enthusiastic salesman who loved building things, William tore into the project despite the terrible financial downturn that followed the panic of 1857. Henry Titus Welles, another early Minneapolis entrepreneur, described this serious national crisis as it played out in Minnesota: "In less than 60 days it became a cloudburst. Eastern creditors called for payment 'in hot haste.' Burbank and Company's express [coaches] carried out as many as $60,000 on some days, but brought nothing back. Our merchants and bankers called for payment by those whom they had habitually trusted. Then customers begged for an extension. Collections were fractional. Finally they ceased. Nobody paid. The money had gone out of the Territory. . . . All through the winter of 1857–58 the majority were sustained by a futile hope, born of past success. They could not believe that real estate had fallen in value."[3]

Not surprisingly, some Minneapolis businessmen threw in the towel and moved back east. Mill Company partners fell behind in their assessments and gave up their shares. At times the company could not pay its taxes. Expenses far exceeded income. The gathering clouds of the Civil War added to economic uncertainty.

As Cadwallader cajoled his creditors into taking minimum payments and beat the bushes for new eastern money, William seemed undaunted. He kept the work going and even attracted tenants—though not nearly enough to recoup the partners' continuing investment. Several small sawmills went up on the dam. Next to it, work began on the waterpower canal, which, by 1859, was 215 feet long, 50 feet wide, and 14 feet deep. That year, it secured its first substantial tenant when local businessmen W. W. Eastman and Paris Gibson opened up the Cataract Flour Mill there. It was a modest start to what would become the thundering heart of a new city.

---

3   Henry Titus Welles, *Autobiography and Reminiscences* (Minneapolis: Marshall Robinson, 1899), 2: 72.

Also in 1859, William married Lizzy in Bangor, and the couple began their journey west together. Passing through Galena, Lizzy ran a Washburn family gauntlet: older brothers Cadwallader and Elihu, stern sister Martha, Elihu's wife, Adele, and Martha's husband, Charles Stephenson. Sister Mary and her family may even have come upriver from Lyons (now Clinton), Iowa. Lizzy passed inspection with flying colors. When the newlyweds arrived at the Falls of St. Anthony, they moved into W. W. Eastman's new hotel, the Nicollet House. Cadwallader and the Mill Company now had all the attractive and energetic representation they needed.

As a married man, William took new action to fill spiritual and social needs in the community. In October 1859, he helped organize a group of like-minded easterners as the First Universalist Society of Minneapolis. Universalism was popular in the northeastern United States, so the new organization provided familiarity as well as comfort to the émigrés. As with William's Passadumkeag Club, this effort attracted future leaders in the community. If Minneapolis was to have an "establishment," William Drew Washburn was one of its earliest architects.

With the beginning of the Civil War in 1861, new passion to preserve the Union settled across the states of the North. Many years later, on the fiftieth anniversary of the fall of Fort Sumter, William recalled the political and commercial excitement when the first call for troops arrived: "Party lines were dropped, business was practically dropped, and the only thoughts were for flag and country."[4] His brothers shared the same experience in Bangor, Augusta, Galena, and La Crosse.

The older Washburn siblings determined to preserve both the Union and the lives of their younger brothers. Israel, Jr., new governor of Maine, led his small state's giant contribution to the war effort. Cadwallader, defeated in his effort to become Wisconsin's newest senator but successful in helping deliver Wisconsin for the Republican Party, raised a regiment of cavalry and took a commission as its colonel. Elihu, a trusted colleague of Abraham Lincoln in Illinois since the early 1840s, became the new president's key ally in Congress. He also promoted the military career of a

---

4   Interview, *Minneapolis Journal*, April 9, 1911.

Galena constituent named Ulysses S. Grant. Elihu helped his younger brother Sam secure a commission in the Union navy.

While Charles and William were fit and of an age to serve, Elihu did his best to protect his two youngest brothers from the war. He helped Charles secure a post as U.S. minister to Paraguay, and he probably was behind Lincoln selecting 30-year-old William surveyor general for Minnesota. William had helped raise a company of infantry from Minneapolis, but with his first child due and his brother's enterprise at the falls teetering in the economic doldrums, he did not sign up himself. Instead, he happily accepted this new assignment.

Being surveyor general meant that William would become familiar with the plats of every new town in the state, as well as every acre of timberland and every navigable or dam-suited stream. Although he had to move his wife and baby to a hotel room in the nearby capital at St. Paul, William would never be too far away to keep an eye on the progress of work at the falls—or to tend to his new lumber business there.

Neither he nor most of the region's entrepreneurs saw anything wrong with taking advantage of war-inflated lumber prices to improve their own enterprises. So, as they made significant patriotic contributions, the Washburn brothers kept up with their business interests as well. In February 1864, for example, when Congressman Elihu was in Washington fighting for Ulysses Grant to be made general of all the Union armies, when Cadwallader, a major general, was swatting flies off the coast of Texas, and when Sid was getting the First National Bank of Hallowell off the ground in Maine, William sold a raft of lumber at Dubuque for $16 per thousand feet—the best price in several years. As investors, all four brothers probably got a piece of the profits from this transaction.[5]

Anticipating the postwar boom in construction, William used income from the mill company during the war to purchase pinelands upriver and

---

5   The Washburn brothers drew careful lines between personal profit and national interest. As governor of Maine, Israel handled record amounts of government funds without blemish. Elihu ceaselessly campaigned against crooked army contractors—including close associates of Union generals. Samuel and Cadwallader opposed illegal cotton trading with the enemy that amounted to $35 million a year through Memphis alone.

to pay crews to cut and float logs down to the sawmills perched on top of the dam. He offered generous leases at the dam to attract other lumber operators. Rising lumber prices helped him launch his own lumber company in 1862. Its centerpiece was the Lincoln Sawmill—the sixth one on the new dam.

William's revenues also helped him obtain real estate in Minneapolis, which he exchanged with his partners for their shares in the mill company. By war's end, the Minneapolis Mill Company had only four owners. William was one of them.

At the same time, he did a good job as surveyor general. He got out and inspected land himself and insisted on accuracy and truth in the surveys that were carried out. He fought unauthorized depredation of prime timberland and kept surveys going despite uncertainties created by the 1862 U.S.–Dakota War. His job also gave him a deep and large view of state affairs and brought him to the attention of a wide range of entrepreneurs across the state.

What probably most delighted William about the survey post was that it allowed him to use the title "General"—which he did for many years thereafter. For three years, from 1861 to 1864, this particular general oversaw the mapping of the state, continued to promote his brother's canal, and, as he could afford it, accumulated upstream timberlands for himself. He even made an investment in the Minnesota Valley Railroad, which headed south and west from St. Paul toward Sioux City, Iowa. (He would finally terminate this investment in 1869, when he became involved in a project with greater potential, the construction of the Northern Pacific Railroad.)

Meanwhile, at the falls, Eastman and Gibson's North Star Woolen Mill opened on the canal in 1864. By the end of the year, with the war winding down, William resigned from the surveyor general's post in St. Paul and returned to Minneapolis. By 1866, he had persuaded no less than nine sawmills to perch next to one another across the top of the dam—each of them connected to upstream booms where the incoming logs floated and to long downstream chutes that moved cut boards past shallow water below the falls.

From the beginning, however, the Minneapolis Mill Company's priority was maximizing the value of its industrial properties along the

Minnesota Historical Society

Sawmills lined the entire west bank dam in 1865, and their web of downstream chutes kept cut boards from getting caught up in the shallows below the dam. During periods of low water, the operations took much-needed water away from enterprises along the canal upstream.

canal. Although water flow at the falls was impressive, it was not limitless. As the canal was extended and more industrial sites were opened up along its course, the company had to purchase and then shut down most of the sawmills atop the dam in order to preserve adequate water levels for their tenants on the canal. By 1876, most of the sawmills were in fact gone.

As either landlord or landlord's agent, William was concerned about this water supply problem for 30 years. Eventually the company would

General Mills Archives

The Washburn B Mill, known as "Washburn's Folly," housed twelve pair of millstones when constructed in 1866 and was designed to produce six hundred barrels of flour a day.

bring in engineer William De la Barre to deepen the canal and improve the headraces to the various mills along it. At the same time William, who was then himself in Congress, would successfully persuade his colleagues to appropriate federal money to build a series of dams on the upstream Mississippi. By holding back the high levels of snowmelt spring runoff, these dams would provide a more consistent level of water at the falls year around and thus preserve the waterpower that was the reason for the city's early existence.

The largest flour mill on the canal in 1866 was the C. C. Washburn flour mill, owned by Cadwallader, with William as a partner. Constructed by Otis Pray, their former neighbor in Livermore, the Washburn B mill was a formidable stone building of six stories, containing 12 pairs of grindstones. Representing the then-incredible investment of $100,000, it could produce 600 barrels of flour a day—far in excess of local demand.

Locals quickly dubbed it "Washburn's Folly." But the naysayers were soon silenced. The Washburns were thinking big, and they knew that the market for their flour stretched far beyond the Upper Mississippi valley.

As early as 1866, waterfall entrepreneurs were shipping 79,000 barrels of flour to New York and Boston.[6] Washburn's Folly paid for itself in two years. The B Mill's success stemmed largely from the Washburns' exemption from paying rent for waterpower, as well as Cadwallader's ability, without leaving his base in La Crosse, Wisconsin, to provide capital and make decisions that put the company at the forefront of milling.

But it didn't start out that way. Perhaps yet unconvinced of William's managerial ability, Cadwallader leased operation of the B Mill to the firm of William Judd and George Brackett, which had already made a success of Eastman's Cataract Mill. This gave restless William time to develop interests above and beyond his brother's businesses. For some years he had been personally acquiring forest lands, and now he had his own sawmill and lumber business. His fortunes were increased in 1867 when the Minneapolis Mill Company issued its first dividend, a generous $20,000, to be split between the now only three remaining partners: Cadwallader, William, and their cousin Dorilus Morrison. (Their 20 percent return on investment did not go unnoticed by other investors, including the brothers John and George Pillsbury, and George's brilliant son, Charles, who were drawn to invest in their first mill here in 1869.)

William also shared his brothers' interest in politics, and he was developing a strong political base among the business leaders of Minneapolis. He served on the school committee, helped build the first library, and invested in the town's first newspaper, the *Minneapolis Tribune*, in 1867.

William's history of multiple investments, frequent new projects, and willingness to let others handle the day-to-day details demonstrated a certain lack of interest in the details of management. Unlike Cadwallader, who concentrated his energies on improving what he had, William's horizons were shorter, and his interest in operations seemed scant. More detrimental, his impatience made him appear deaf

---

6   Jocelyn Wills, Boosters, *Hustlers, and Speculators: Entrepreneurial Culture and the Rise of Minneapolis and St. Paul, 1849–1883* (St. Paul: Minnesota Historical Press, 2005), 128.

to the suggestions of others. He was perceived by some as inflexible and difficult in work matters.[7]

Cadwallader, reelected to his seat in Congress in 1866, had to cut back his visits to the falls. When William Eastman's west-side water tunnel began adding greatly to the water supply at the canal, Cadwallader became unsatisfied with the level of production at the B Mill. William suggested Cad bring in veteran mill manager George H. Christian in 1868 to replace William's old friend, George Brackett. Cadwallader agreed. Brackett and Judd, who were preoccupied with building railroads anyway, ended their management of the B Mill, and George Christian took over operations.

Minnesota Historical Society

George Christian, who was hired by Cadwallader Washburn at William's suggestion, replaced William in the management of the B Mill within a year. He was instrumental in introducing the "purifier" machine.

In Christian, the Washburns found not only a good manager, but an open-minded leader who encouraged the first of several technological breakthroughs for which Cadwallader became famous. Most important was the middlings purifier, an ingenious machine which separated the hard shell and bran of the wheat berry from its soft interior. The resulting process turned Minnesota's cold-climate specialty, hard winter wheat, into the finest white flour in the world. The company began calling its product "New Process" flour.

As their product improved, so did demand. But so also did management tensions between Christian and William Washburn. Within a year, Christian was in revolt, and he told Cadwallader that one of them

---

7   The General Mills archives in Minneapolis holds papers from John Crosby IV and Gisbert Van Steenwick, Jr. (son of Cadwallader Washburn's banker) indicating that among the people who had business disagreements with William were future managers John Crosby, James S. Bell, C. C. Bovey, and banker Gisbert Van Steenwick, Sr.

had to go, Cadwallader, apparently aware of William's shortcomings, chose Christian and removed his brother from management of the C. C. Washburn Company.

The incident is revealing. William had been superb as Cadwallader's front man, but their operation had moved into a new phase, where operating efficiency was needed as much as promotional enthusiasm. Cadwallader was a pragmatic businessman who combined vision with dogged persistence. William shared the vision but was easily bored. As the business, and the stakes, grew, Cadwallader turned elsewhere for the people he needed. When he got them, he backed them up—even against his own kin.

To be sure, William was not left high and dry. He retained his interest in the Minneapolis Mill Company, under whose auspices the dam and canal had been built and which produced a growing flow of dividends from businesses renting the land and waterpower. He still had his pinelands and his rent-free sawmill. And he had his own ambitions.

Now William dreamed of adding his own flour business to his lumber company. He had his eye on a site 20 miles upstream from Minneapolis, closer to the forests, in Anoka. He dreamed of building a large sawmill and a flour mill there, where the Rum River flowed into the Mississippi. He even dreamed of persuading someone to build a railroad there to serve the area's manufacturers.

Determined to move ahead, in 1867 William established his new company, the W. D. Washburn Company, folded his Lincoln sawmill at the Falls of St. Anthony into it, and began plans for Anoka operations. Early on he hired a bookkeeper named William Dinsmore Hale, who was also from Maine. Hale had had a distinguished army career during the war, starting as a sergeant and ending as a major, a title he used for the rest of his life. After a year of cotton farming in Arkansas, Major Hale came to Minneapolis as an agent for the Freedmen's Bureau. At W. D. Washburn Company, he received several promotions, moved over to become agent for the waterpower company in 1872, and became William's partner there in 1874. William turned the entire management of that enterprise over to him in 1879.

In some ways Hale's subsequent lifetime of closely working with William challenges the claim that William was an impossible workmate. Hale apparently earned William's trust early on and he stayed close at hand, a devoted friend and partner through the thick and thin of flour milling and railroad adventures. Hale was a strong political lieutenant, as well. Not long after William was elected a U.S. senator, Hale was appointed postmaster of Minneapolis, the most powerful political job in the state. In an era when every new settlement needed a post office, nobody commanded more patronage than the Minneapolis postmaster.

At Anoka, William Washburn, who was now determined to succeed on his own, pursued his ambitious undertaking. First, in 1870 he purchased a small sawmill there. With Cadwallader's benign approval and multiple short-term loans from brothers Sid and Elihu, as well, William then built an enormous new sawmill. Already owning thousands of acres of timberlands upstream, he

Minnesota Historical Society

The steady and quiet Major William D. Hale gave William Washburn the manager he needed to build and run successful sawmill and flour milling enterprises.

opened a new mill complex in 1872 that included a planing mill and dry houses to handle his logs. By the end of the year he had two hundred employees producing 100,000 feet of lumber a day. (Some 150 miles down the Mississippi River, Cadwallader followed this example at his own La Crosse, Wisconsin, sawmill.)[8]

In 1873, William turned back to the flour business. In Minneapolis he built a new flour mill, the Palisade Mill, with partners Rufus Stevens and

---

8   The Lacrosse Lumber Company mill at one time employed four hundred men and produced more shingles than any other operation in the Upper Mississippi Valley. In 1873, the company opened up a large lumber yard at Louisiana, Missouri. The company still exists, operating 13 lumber yards across central Missouri and southern Illinois.

Leonard Day. Perhaps on Cad's advice, he turned management over to Stevens and Day, and for the next 11 years, William enjoyed a share of the profits without having to worry about day-to-day details.

In his seemingly charmed life, William had had few serious financial fears, unlike his older brothers. He had always found investors, and Cadwallader had always backed him up if William was over-extended. By the approach of summer in 1873, while Cadwallader was becoming graver than usual, William blithely continued borrowing and spending money in all directions, with little apparent thought of consequences if his lenders suddenly had to cut their credit short. That year William invested in Minneapolis's first street railway company.

But trouble lay ahead for the Washburns—and for the entire Upper Mississippi valley. First, there was a family death, when brother Israel, customs collector in Portland, Maine, and his wife Maud visited Minneapolis to see their son Charles, who was ill. Maud, in her turn, took ill, and in August she died.

Then, on October 1, railroad baron Jay Cooke's Philadelphia bank, which held the bonds of many of the new railroads in the Upper Midwest, failed. This set in motion a panic and economic collapse that left few in Minneapolis unaffected. Speculators were caught short. Over-extended railroads including the Northern Pacific went bankrupt, and the economy sank into the most severe depression in the country's history. It was 1857 all over again. Money dried up, banks called in loans, borrowers defaulted, and the value of every investment plummeted. Cadwallader, who was deeply obligated to lenders and investors, called on every resource and barely persuaded his creditors to hold off so he could stay afloat.

William, who was as casual about debts as other details, was caught seriously short of funds. His creditors, under threat of sinking themselves, would not be put off. William had to open up his books to them and bare every asset he owned. Although it stretched them fearfully, his brothers Elihu and Cadwallader stood by him and guaranteed William's most critical obligations. He closed the W. D. Washburn Company, reorganized, and then started all over again under a new name, the Washburn Mill Company. The fledgling street railway company in Minneapolis failed.

By year's end, and as colleagues went bankrupt all around him, William had lost about half his assets. But he still had plenty and Cadwallader guaranteed them all. William acknowledged to Elihu in December that, throughout the crisis, "Cad stood by me like a hero."[9]

The gory details published in the *Northwestern Miller* provide impressive evidence of William's success in his 16 years in Minneapolis. Even after being stripped of more than a half million dollars in assets, he still owned a "magnificent" residence, his mill and property at Anoka, the planing mill, 11,000 pineland acres in three states, between eight and ten million feet of sawn lumber, and his stock in the Minneapolis Mill Company.[10]

While Cadwallader came out of the experience vowing never to go into debt again, William seemed unaffected. He found it easy to return to Maine for a reunion of his Bowdoin class. The following summer he finished a letter to Sid, who had dozens of short-term loans out to him, advising his older brother to "Keep cool." He described his own household—now including five children—as "all foxy and well."[11]

Perhaps to "cool" William's own optimism, Elihu invited the whole family in 1875 to France, where Elihu was in his fifth year as the American minister. Leaving their families together there, the brothers traveled to Egypt, where the great French promoter, Ferdinand DeLesseps, had just completed a new wonder, the Suez Canal. It is questionable whether William was cooled off or heated up by this experience, since he headed back to Minneapolis burning with his old energy and optimism intact.

With the possible exception of flour milling, William found Minneapolis in economic shambles when he returned. Production had slowed on their waterpower canal, and Cadwallader's nearly-completed A Mill, with 41 runs of stones and capacity to produce 1,200 barrels of flour a day, was once again putting him far ahead of any visible demand for his product. An original canal tenant, the flamboyant Paris Gibson, had gone out of business completely, leaving an empty flour mill and a cloud of

---

9   William D. Washburn to Elihu B. Washburn, December 6, 1874, Washburn Family Papers.

10 *Northwestern Miller*, October 27, 1874.

11 William Drew Washburn to Algernon Sidney Washburn, August 4, 1874, A. S. Washburn Papers, Duke University, Durham, North Carolina.

unpaid debts, and was said to be raising sheep in Montana. The Gibson's other property on the canal, the North Star Woolen Mill, wobbled along until 1876, when it declared bankruptcy. Recognizing the inherent viability of the company, William and his uncle Dorillus Morrison stepped in on behalf of the Mill Company, bought North Star, and found managers for it who restored it to health. The hugely overextended Northern Pacific Railroad had built poorly in its race to keep its government land grants and, unable to meet its obligations, had crashed spectacularly. (The subsequent availability of its St. Paul and Pacific subsidiary would furnish the start for James J. Hill's career in railroading.) William, however, albeit on a reduced scale, was able to keep his businesses going and his head above water. Benefiting from Minneapolis Mill dividends, he put his sawmills and lumberyards back into operation, and his eye continued to rove for new opportunities. He even installed one of Alexander Graham Bell's new telephone lines so he could talk from Minneapolis to his Anoka sawmill.[12]

In 1875, with real estate operator Thomas Lowry, William bought a piece of the city's second street railway, a horse-drawn operation just 4 1/2 miles in length. In 1878, he started the city's first evening newspaper, the *Minneapolis Journal*, which would become an important adjunct to his political career. In 1881, with Otis A. Pray, he founded the Minnesota Brush Electric Company, which supplied Minneapolis with the first electric streetlights in the country. As these infant enterprises sputtered to life, their future was uncertain, but the economy was improving. All three, as it turned out, would prosper.

When Cadwallader's mill manager George Christian retired, Cadwallader was desperate for someone he could trust to keep an eye on things. He brought William back into his flour partnership in 1877, but the reinstatement was a short one. Not long afterwards, Cadwallader asked the competent John Crosby to take over his milling operations at the Falls of St. Anthony, and William was dropped again in 1879.

With Hale running things well in Anoka and the new Washburn-Crosby Company in good hands at the falls, Young Rapid badly needed new excitement. He found it next in the field of transportation.

---

12   Wills, *Boosters*, 207.

The Northwest frontier had originally been settled by water, with rivers providing the primary transportation within Minnesota. Roads, including the primitive supply track to Canada, were inadequate to support the amount of goods being produced by the booming new industries at the falls.

Now the railroads were coming. Not only would they bisect the landscape with ribbons of steel, punctuated every few miles by water tanks and station houses. They would lace those ribbons with telegraph lines to bring instant communication across the vast land. They would bring people to work, lumber to build the towns, and merchandise for commerce. They would also bring farmers, many of them immigrants, and provide a year-round way to move crops to markets hundreds of miles away.

Railroad cars rolling on low-friction tracks across level country represented by far the easiest and least expensive way to propel heavy loads across the countryside. By 1880, skilled railroad builder James J. Hill could haul an eight-hundred-ton train with one primitive locomotive. (Two decades later Hill could carry a ton of freight across a mile of track for one-quarter of a penny.)[13] Railroads, millers, and even farmers would soon begin to add garlands of grain elevators at railroad switching points that not only provided farmers with convenient places to sell their crops, but provided buyers with a means of storing them while waiting out low grain prices.

At the other end of their business, millers improved their product, and demand for their flour rose across the country, creating demand for inexpensive, reliable transportation. Despite the wreckage of failed railroad investments across the Upper Midwest and the millers' extreme reluctance to enter into this business they knew nothing about, they were about to make railroads part of their business. Their need supplied the perfect venue for William's next career.

---

13   Albro Martin, *James J. Hill and the Opening of the Northwest* (New York: Oxford University Press, 1976), 116, 287, and 431.

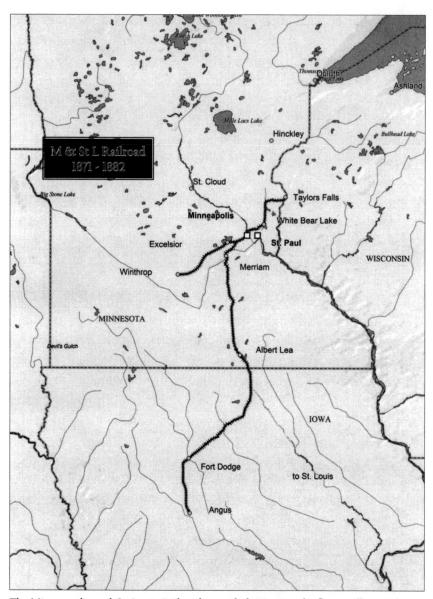

The Minneapolis and St. Louis Railroad provided Minneapolis flour millers with independent rail links via White Bear Lake to Duluth and via Albert Lea to St. Louis. Extensions to Taylors Falls, Winthrop, and the coal fields in Iowa came later.

3

The Call of the Iron Horse
1869–1882

The train crew gaped into the early dawn. Before them, the track just stopped. The rails they had been using yesterday were suddenly gone. The entire track had been taken up during the night, and now there was no sign of it. It looked as if the freight they were carrying would have to go another way. The millers of Minneapolis—for it was their flour that was being delayed—would have a fresh reason to be frustrated about bringing their product to market.

Back in his office that afternoon, one of those millers would write furiously to his brother, also a miller. "Sherburne Merrill is a he-devil," William Washburn scribbled to his brother Cadwallader in Wisconsin. "We have got to have other rail connections or we are gone up."[14]

Sherburne Merrill, and his boss, Alexander Mitchell, in Milwaukee had never in fact been friends of Minnesota's flour millers. Since the late 1860s, their railroad, the Chicago, Milwaukee and St. Paul, or Milwaukee Road (the first to provide eastbound service from Minneapolis), had set a rate schedule that expressly favored Milwaukee's millers. Not only that, but they had lately built two huge elevators there and were paying wheat farmers in a southern Minnesota 10 cents more per bushel than the millers in Minneapolis could offer.

Minneapolis millers had one other rail carrier to transport their product, but it was no better. The Chicago and Northwestern Railroad seemed indifferent to delays caused by unavailable equipment, limited track and switch capacity, and clogged switchyards in Chicago. Eastbound cargo sometimes waited days to be transferred to eastbound lines.

---

14 William Drew Washburn to Cadwallader C. Washburn, May 6 and 10, 1869, Washburn Family Papers.

Shipping through the port of Duluth (shown here around 1875), though open only about seven months a year, represented a desirable alternative to Minneapolis millers with cargo bound for the East Coast.

It had taken time for these "foreign" railroad operators to realize the business potential of the mills at the Falls of St. Anthony. Instead, the operators' Minnesota investments went through the capital at St. Paul, the head of navigation on the Mississippi River. St. Paul was the source for securing land grants. St. Paul was bigger than Minneapolis and growing faster. It offered a shorter and less expensive route to Duluth, the summertime shipping point of choice on Lake Superior. Not surprisingly St. Paul was Minnesota's early railroad hub.

Nobody in Minneapolis knew much about the railroad business in 1869, and millers such as Cadwallader Washburn seemed disinclined to learn. But William, who loved building things that went fast, was interested. In 1870, having gotten out of his investment in the Minnesota Valley Railroad, he joined his friend George Brackett and others investing in a construction company working on the Northern Pacific's Minnesota Division. Perhaps to their surprise, they won the contract to build the road's first 50-mile section on the route from Duluth west to the Dakota border. Once completed, this line would provide a direct link between the burgeoning wheat belt along the Red River and ships headed to mills as far east as Buffalo, New York.

The project went well, and William's enthusiasm for a millers' railroad increased. Thanks to a big infusion of Philadelphia investment money from Jay Cooke and his friends, the St. Paul and Duluth line had just been completed. Its management was eager to provide freight service for whoever needed it from St. Paul to the docks on Lake Superior.

The Philadelphians built a station on their new line at White Bear Lake, just north of St. Paul and only 13 miles from the mills at the Falls of St. Anthony. Not only that, another new line, the St. Paul and Pacific, was being funded by Dutch money to run westward directly from St. Paul to the Red River. As the grain supply increased in the West and flour orders increased in the East, even reluctant Cadwallader admitted the importance of having his freight in friendly hands.

So millers in Minneapolis pored over their maps and decided to dip their collective toe in the railroad business. Cadwallader, William, friend Henry Welles, and a half dozen others dusted off an old charter and got permission from the state legislature. In May 1871, they incorporated a line they called the Minneapolis and Duluth. Local money was scarce, but with support from Philadelphia investors, the millers quickly completed a link from the falls to White Bear Lake, celebrating in July with an eight-car special train, five hundred guests, and a brass band. William, who spoke to guests at a celebratory picnic, gave credit to the Philadelphians and noted that "we shall transfer the road to them, and I can assure you gentlemen that they will run it on liberal principles."[15] During the summer

---

15   Frank P. Donovan, *Mileposts on the Prairie* (New York: Simmons-Boardman, 1950), 25.

months anyway, the millers now had a more friendly way to ship their product north to Duluth and then east via the Great Lakes.

Minneapolis's millers were happy to turn over actual operation of the Minneapolis and Duluth Railroad to Cooke and crew, although William remained titular president. This was just as well, since light traffic forced William to cut in half his optimistic first-day August schedule of four trains a day each way.

Gaining confidence, William and Cadwallader determined to offer millers a second railroad project, the Minneapolis and St. Louis Railroad. Their goal was not just a small summertime link to Lake Superior, but a year-round rail outlet heading south. It would run to Albert Lea, Minnesota, and to links through Iowa south to St. Louis, steering well clear of the discriminatory and delay-prone Chicago roads.

It proved expensive to build the Minneapolis and St. Louis route —it was longer and harder than the White Bear Lake link—and William the evangelist was never William the day-to-day manager. During its first year, construction inched slowly over the ravines, hills, and rivers south of Minneapolis. When in November 1871 the line reached its first major goal at Sioux City Junction 28 miles south of Minneapolis, William ordered up another special train, brass band, and celebration. Among the patriotic speeches extolling the power of the railroad to unify the country was an offering from one Henry Young of Chaska, who enthused, "No more Dutchmen, no more Norwegians, no more Frenchmen, no more Irishmen, no more Yermans, no more Yews, nodding but Amerigans."[16]

The lease with Cooke's people had an adverse impact on the line the following year. Rate wars between Cooke's Duluth line and Mitchell's Milwaukee Road line chewed into profits and bled off construction money. So did the maintenance costs to keep one section on the route to White Bear Lake from sinking into a swamp. Throughout 1872, not one mile of the 80 remaining miles from Sioux City Junction—soon renamed Merriam Junction—to Albert Lea was completed. The year was one long struggle to maintain schedules, meet payrolls, and keep trains from tipping over.

The Minneapolis and St. Louis was far short of its intended link-up with lines to Missouri when financial disaster overtook Jay Cooke in September

---

16 Donovan, *Mileposts*, 30.

1873. Cooke's over-extended amalgamation of Minnesota railroads suddenly collapsed like the house of cards it was. His dramatic fall in fact dragged the entire United States into the greatest economic depression in its history. Damage to the Upper Mississippi valley was particularly acute. Within months Cooke defaulted on his railroad bonds, and in 1874 control of both the Minneapolis and Duluth and the Minneapolis and St. Louis reverted to its shareholders, led by the reluctant Washburn brothers, Henry Welles, and construction contractor Robert B. Langdon.

To keep going, the Minneapolis and St. Louis took over the Minneapolis and Duluth and issued new stock, most of which was taken by William, who became president. Bankruptcy was close, and actually claimed two of William's fellow directors and tenants on the falls waterpower canal, Paris Gibson and Richard Mendenhall. The lucky Washburn crown prince, however, backed by Cadwallader, stayed afloat. So did their railroad—barely. By 1874, the entire Minneapolis and St. Louis organization amounted to one paid officer and 42 miles of rickety 49-pound track with little ballast, plus four locomotives, five passenger cars, and 68 pieces of freight equipment, mostly leased from Cooke's bankrupt Northern Pacific.[17] The company produced no income in excess of operating expenses. Their grain storage capacity was six times less than their Northern Pacific, Manitoba, Milwaukee, and Chicago and Northwestern competitors.

Railroad dreams nevertheless continued to flicker. In 1872, William, with two other Minneapolis and St. Louis directors, had joined six other local businessmen to form a group they called the Minneapolis Board of Trade.[18] Members met frequently to discuss business affairs in the young city. The next spring, William invited his brother Israel, visiting from Maine, to speak to the group. Israel had something to say. In remarks titled "From the Northwest to the Sea," the bespectacled former governor from

---

17   Stanley, Jr., remembered his grandfather William instructing crews to skip careful grading and simply lay the ties on the ground and spike the rails well enough to support a single engine to pull a single gondola car of grain back to Minneapolis. Personal reminiscence, 1993, Washburn Family Papers.

18   The Board of Trade is not to be confused with the Minneapolis Chamber of Commerce, established in 1881, which became the Minneapolis Grain Exchange in 1948.

Maine Historical Society

Oldest Washburn brother Israel Washburn, Jr., former governor and collector of customs at Portland, planted the seed for the Soo Line Railroad in an 1873 speech.

Maine gave his audience that day in April 1873 a railroad vision that would last for many years to come.

"Gabe," as his brothers called him, was small and somewhat rounded, perhaps by his good living as Maine's highest paid federal employee, the collector of customs at Portland. Having served 10 years as Bangor's congressman, spearheading the formation of the Republican Party, he had been an effective and popular governor. Appointed by President Lincoln to his customs post in 1863, he had tirelessly promoted the shipping advantages of the huge harbor at Portland with its direct railroad connection to Montreal, Canada. Well aware of the steady influx of new immigrants across the northern prairies and of the excellent prospects for New Process flour, Israel called his audience's attention to the map. With quiet logic and Washburn intensity, he pointed to a huge shortcoming of all the existing Minneapolis rail routes to the East. None followed the shortest path.

The straightest, shortest, and, therefore, cheapest route east from Minneapolis was a nearly straight line along the 45th parallel. Whether the destination was New York, Boston, or Portland, the shortest route crossed the Upper Michigan peninsula and Canada. This all-weather shipping route would be more than two hundred miles shorter than shipping via Chicago. In addition, the route to Europe from his own port of Portland, Maine, was another three hundred miles shorter than it was from New York City. The Canadians would be eager partners. Why not, the customs collector asked, build your own direct line?

Freight rates were figured in terms of weight and miles. Given the hundreds—soon to be thousands—of barrels that each miller would be shipping east every day, the savings in freight costs represented by the shorter route, plus the friendly and well-capitalized lines on the Canadian side of the border, caught the attention of every miller in Israel's audience. Despite the skepticism of the press—the *Northwestern Miller* called Israel's idea "the north pole railroad"—the seeds of the future Soo Line were planted that day.

Israel had lit the flame. Though he himself would not live to see the road built, over the next 10 years of difficult times that flame would not be extinguished. In 1888, Minnesota flour via Soo Line box cars would ship directly from Minneapolis to Europe through his customs house in Portland.

After the collapse of 1873, grasshopper invasions on midwestern farms and the fear of being straight-jacketed by state laws setting freight rates, as well as national economic malaise, scared eastern investors away from new railroad construction for years . Despite this, William lost none of his enthusiasm for an independent railroad. In October he spoke bluntly about the millers' transport problems, telling a newspaper reporter that the railroad business serving Minneapolis "was controlled by a set of sharks and speculators, men who have amassed fortunes not in legitimate businesses but by a systematic robbery of the people."[19] Amid the 1873 crash and the recent national Crédit Mobilier railroad scandal, this rhetoric struck a common chord among both the millers and the farmers across the countryside who supplied them.

In 1876, with the local economy still prostrate, all Minneapolis flour on the Minneapolis and St. Louis went north via White Bear Lake to Duluth. By 1878, the railroads had become an integral part of the milling operations. That was the year that the M&StL built the first railroad trestles directly along the city's riverfront "mill row," a significant accomplishment by Cadwallader, who had managed to purchase all the land around the mills for tracks and trestles.

---

19   Interview with William D. Washburn, *Minneapolis Tribune*, October 28, 1873. The decade was marked by the political struggle between farmers wanting equitable freight rates and railroads needing to offer varying rates that would attract big-volume customers.

The Minneapolis and St. Louis railroad's most valuable asset was access to the Minneapolis mills. Although millers only reluctantly entered the railroad business, railroads became an integral part of their operation. The elevated trestles along "Mill Row," shown in 1890, left other transportation to and from the mills in the shadows underneath.

By elevating the tracks on trestles to the same level where the 195-pound barrels of flour came out of the mills, millers could greatly reduce loading time and effort. In short order, all of the feeder tracks in the mill district were elevated to form a continuous platform from one mill to another and from one side of the row to the other. Not one horse or wagon was to be seen, as all drayage traffic operated in the shadows below the trestles.

Even with Philadelphians out of the picture, the dream of a rail outlet to the south persisted along Minneapolis's mill row. William, with customary energy, undertook a furious search for financing the M&StL. He knocked on all sorts of doors. From small town councils out on the prairie toward Albert Lea to the big banks in London, he went with hat in hand. All the while William was personally so short on cash that Cadwallader was paying the assessments on his brother's M&StL bonds.

Slowly the desperately needed funding came in, and construction sputtered along. In November 1877 the brothers got their railroad line completed to Albert Lea

Hennepin County Library

The 1878 explosion that ruined Cadwallader Washburn's A Mill wiped out half of the flour production in Minneapolis. After a two-year battle with insurance companies, Cadwallader prevailed, and production doubled by 1880.

just as Iowans brought their line up from the south to connect with it. True to form, William arranged a big celebration to mark the occasion, taking the official train down to straddle the state line, one car in Minnesota and the other in Iowa. For the third time—topping the previous occasions at White Bear Lake and at Sioux City Junction—William announced from the banquet table that it was the happiest day of his life. And it probably was.

Both Washburn brothers had to spend heavily to protect their investment. By 1879, they would own five times as much M&StL stock as they had two years earlier. This proved too much for Cadwallader, who was sick and preoccupied with insurance battles after a disastrous explosion and fire destroyed his A Mill and several others in 1878. He determined to leave the railroad business even though soaring grain production in the Red River Valley was bringing about frenetic railroad construction there, and Minneapolis flour production was skyrocketing, nearing one million barrels in 1877. Three years later Minneapolis millers were producing two million barrels a year.

Increased production meant more than 10 thousand carloads a year of freight business for railroads serving the city. This volume rekindled the interest of out-of-state operators, and moguls in Chicago and Milwaukee began to move in to buy up key connecting lines that Minneapolis millers depended upon. In 1879, even the friendly St. Paul and Duluth Railroad fell under the Milwaukee Road's control. Once again millers were dealing with Sherburne Merrill, and without warning, the Washburns found their freight rates to Duluth increased by 14 cents a barrel. A battle ensued.

Cadwallader Washburn had wanted out of the railroad business, but he and William knew the best defense was a good offense. Accordingly they announced a plan to build their own railroad to Lake Superior. They would extend from their railhead at White Bear Lake northeastward across the St. Croix River at Taylors Falls and then north up the other side—all the way to the lake at Ashland, Wisconsin. If built, this road would provide the millers not only with a completely independent route to Lake Superior, but an independent loading facility for ships carrying flour to Cleveland and Buffalo. Throughout 1879, the Washburns carried out surveys across the 26 miles from White Bear Lake to Taylors Falls, and the next year the Minneapolis and St. Louis (M&StL), with William as president, began construction.

Realizing that Minneapolis millers were serious, the St. Paul and Duluth Railroad finally agreed to talk. Sherburne Merrill and Cadwallader Washburn hammered out a deal for future rates on the Milwaukee Road, and the St. Paul and Duluth also came to terms. The millers could use the tracks to Duluth for five years at the annual rent of $58,000, a sum far smaller than the cost of building another line. The Washburns' new rail line from Wyoming, Minnesota, to Taylors Falls, was completed in November 1880, but it never went any further. A five-year truce between the giants reigned, marking Cadwallader Washburn's final contribution to the millers' railroading struggles.

The deal also brought relative health to the M&StL. By 1878, the company had secured its long-sought connections to St. Louis and was beginning to recoup construction expenses. It could buy new equipment and pay interest on its bonds, which were selling nearly at par. The

Hennepin County Library

Extensive barriers of rock along the route from White Bear Lake to Taylors Falls, made construction expensive, but in order to get equitable freight rates in the 1870s, the Washburns had to demonstrate that they were serious about constructing a line from Minneapolis to Lake Superior.

M&StL was even building new lines. One reached westward to the resort hamlet of Excelsior on Lake Minnetonka, and by 1881 this line reached out to new wheat fields 69 miles from Minneapolis to Winthrop.

Cadwallader's milling business was doing even better. Following George Christian's retirement back in 1875, Cadwallader, who was even less able to tend personally to his businesses, went through several combinations of managers for his flour mills. Elected governor of Wisconsin in 1871 and preoccupied for more than a decade with trying to get elected to the U.S. Senate, he wanted energetic people he could trust in Minneapolis. He briefly re-enlisted William but then Cad found the man he really wanted—manufacturer John Crosby from Bangor. The writing was on the wall for William, even though Crosby was married to William's sister-in-law Olive Muzzy. Within months of Crosby's arrival in Minneapolis, there was another management collision, another ultimatum, and another termination. William was out of Cadwallader's flour business for the second time. Washburn-Crosby went on to flourish without him.

Although William was having success with the M&StL, a weary Cadwallader still wanted out. He threatened to sell his stock to the hated Chicago and Northwestern road. William rushed to New York, where legend had it that he had a heated confrontation with his brother in the middle of the street. Cadwallader was adamant. He was sick and he was tired. He had used the last of his energy to get a phalanx of insurance companies to pay up for the flour mills wrecked in the great A Mill explosion on May 2, 1878. Now, under Crosby's management and the introduction of more new technology, his rebuilt mills had never done better.

Cadwallader finally sold out his majority share of the M&StL to a group of sympathetic New York bankers. They held on for a couple of years, but by 1881 the Minneapolis board members —H.T. Welles, J. K. Sidle, and the faithful Major Hale—were gradually replaced with men known to be sympathetic to a new combination of the Omaha (the Chicago, St. Paul, Minneapolis and Omaha) and the Rock Island (the Chicago, Rock Island and Pacific) line. William, who had been serving in Congress since 1876, was often absent, a figurehead president, outnumbered and outvoted. By May 1882, the month Cadwallader died, control of the Minneapolis and St. Louis passed to the outsiders. William was replaced as president, although he retained his stock and held a seat on the board of the Omaha line. Reflective of his life-long pattern, he had provided the inspiration and enthusiasm to get the enterprise started, only to be replaced by the hard-headed managers needed to keep it successful.

William's history with the M&StL would foreshadow his history with the Soo Line. From concept to execution, he was crucial. His salesmanship and emotion perfectly reflected the spirit of the millers and their city. His outrage at "foreign" railroads was their outrage. His vision of independence was their vision. He ignored every financial crisis with almost light-hearted disregard and greeted every advance with a joyous celebration. But he was little involved in day-to-day management details, operations he left to others. During the last three years of his involvement with the M&StL, William was fortunate that among the people taking care of the details for him was Chief Engineer W. W. Rich. Rich was a quietly efficient man would do great things for William in the years ahead.

By 1880, Minneapolis mills were producing 30,000 barrels of flour every day. Every mill had contractual obligations to deliver products to buyers far, far away—in the East and overseas. As their businesses grew, the millers became increasingly aware of their continuing vulnerability to the whims of railroads whose priorities lay elsewhere.

From St. Paul, mogul James J. Hill dropped the final straw when he connected a link of his St. Paul, Minneapolis and Manitoba Road from the western Minnesota town of St. Cloud through woods to the Duluth line at Hinckley, Minnesota. This link gave wheat farmers in the rich Red River Valley another direct outlet to Lake Superior that bypassed Minneapolis completely. Minneapolis millers knew losing this raw wheat would be devastating, and William interrupted a vacation at Arkansas's hot baths to write, "Such action . . . will cause a damage in our two cities that cannot be measured."[20]

Still, the millers hesitated. In the four years between 1878 and 1882, William Washburn had been removed from the management of two of the city's leading firms: the Washburn-Crosby flour mills (twice), and the M&StL railroad. In addition, railroads were still the riskiest investment imaginable. The money needed up front was enormous, and the landscape was littered with the wreckage of hundreds, if not thousands, of railroad schemes that never got built, that went broke, that were repossessed by the banks, or that were swallowed up by bigger players for mere cents on the dollar. Those big players—the survivors of 1873—were among the toughest competitors in the world. Men like Sherborn Merrill, Jim Hill, Cornelius Vanderbilt,

---

20   Martin, *J. J. Hill*, 361.

and young William Van Horne were giving no quarter as they rammed their rails across the countryside.

William Washburn knew all this, but he was not afraid. His own businesses had never been better—or more in need of independent rail service. He had flour mills in Minneapolis and upriver in Anoka plus a huge sawmill in Anoka and thousands of acres of Minnesota timberlands to feed it. From the grave, Cadwallader, dead in 1882, had put him back into the management of Washburn-Crosby milling to represent the interests of the family during the five years it took to settle Cad's estate. With business booming again, William judged that the investment climate was ripe for the realization of the millers' long-held dream of their own railroad east. The railroading fire had returned to his eye.

4

The Challenge
1883–1886

In 1898 Henry Titus Welles, looking over the thundering city that Minneapolis had become, wrote about the Soo Line railroad: "General Washburn and Mr. Thomas Lowry and Mr. Langdon and others carried forward the work through much tribulation and with a skill and fortitude that ought to give them a world-wide fame . . . Too much cannot be said in their praise, and I devoutly hope that prosperity will be their ultimate reward. Less than ten men built the modern Minneapolis—Washburn, Lowry, Martin, Eastman, Morrison, the Days, the Pillsburys. To their genius and indomitable perseverance not only the city but the whole state is indebted."[21]

The words, written by a man who was there, were about William, not Cadwallader. They summarized Young Rapid's reputation in the city and the state as the century drew to a close. That reputation came from his greatest challenge and triumph.

On a late fall day in 1883, in the heart of the forest of northern Wisconsin, two figures toiled through the silent landscape. The country was heavily wooded, gently rolling country—typical of glacial terrain. The lowlands were full of water—swamps, ponds, south-flowing streams, and, occasionally, a substantial river. High ground consisted of rounded hills with a few rocky outcrops on their windswept heights. The trampers' goal for this day was the high point of a hill between a small stream called Pokegama Creek and the Chippewa River. As they gained it, the two men paused. The river stretched below them, 100 feet wide and deep. The

---

21   Henry Titus Welles, *Autobiography and Reminiscences, Vol. 2: 1853-1898* (Marshall Robinson, Minneapolis, 1899), p 147. Welles was William's partner and financial backer in the Soo Line adventure.

leader carefully measured the elevation of the land where he stood. It was 225 feet above the Chippewa in front of him and almost that much back down to the drainage behind him.

They had been tramping eastward across empty country for several days. One figure, an Indian guide, was bowed under a large pack. The other figure was a stocky man, wearing high-laced leather boots and lugging a well-used surveyor's theodolite over one shoulder. His face was weather-beaten and whiskered. He was not interested in the scenery. He paused on each slope they crossed, taking readings of the steepness of the ground. As he crisscrossed the thickly overgrown terrain, he paused frequently to make notations in a worn notebook. He had a determined look to him, and he was very thorough. He would continue his survey of this ground for two full days, covering all the approaches to the west bank of the Chippewa.

The man was on a mission. He had been asked to put a dollar figure on an absurd dream to build a railroad across this country. This man's attention was on the slope of the ground—always the slope. Was there a route across these barriers with a grade that primitive wood-burning locomotives, each hauling strings of heavily-loaded freight cars, could handle? He needed a grade of no more than one foot up or down per 100 feet, a track with no sharp curves, and the straightest and shortest path possible. For every watercourse, the chosen path had to lead to the best spot for a bridge. Each bridge would have to withstand the challenges that ice jams, log jams, or spring floods could throw at it. The man quietly calculated amounts of earth to be moved, rock to be blasted, timber to be cut, pilings to be driven, and bridges to be built. He thought about labor and resources. Getting a railroad across this territory could not be done in anything like the three miles per day that James J. Hill's and Cornelius Van Horne's contractors were doing just then across the prairies of Dakota and Saskatchewan. This would be much harder than that, much slower, and much more expensive.

The man and his guide had measured their way here from a way station on the Omaha railroad back at Turtle Lake, now 40 miles behind them. Ahead, beyond the river, lay another 50 miles of country to explore. Only after they had examined it all would they emerge from the woods.

From another tiny way station, the surveyor would telegraph his patrons back in Minneapolis that he was alive and well, that he had completed the first phase of his job. It would take him three more weeks to deliver his report in person.

The surveyor's name was Watson Wellman Rich. Because of his record in the Union army during the Civil War, he was most often referred to simply as "Captain Rich." He was a fact-oriented man, but it would be his fate to make a dream—an outlandish dream—come true. He would have the chief responsibility for a project that had been shimmering in the imaginations of its boosters in Minneapolis for more than 10 years.

His patrons were successful businessmen, but none would be considered wealthy by eastern standards. Far from big money centers like New York and Chicago, the men had flourished independently—as flour millers, real estate speculators, lumbermen, wholesale grocers, and frontier bankers. They had prospered as Minneapolis had mushroomed into a small city around them. They were strong and confident in their businesses.

But they knew nothing about building railroads. They had just survived 10 long years of down times after the economic catastrophe of 1873—a disaster they felt had been caused by eastern speculators far removed from their world and far beyond their control. Now, in a rush of enthusiasm, they had overcome years of well-founded hesitation. They had joined together to try and throw a railroad across five hundred miles of wilderness that none of them had ever seen. The southern half of Minnesota, including the cities of St. Paul and Minneapolis, had been populated by people who came up the Mississippi River from St. Louis and Illinois. Aside from the lumbermen and sawmill operators along the tributary streams that fed the Mississippi, few knew much about the interior of northern Wisconsin. In the rush to settle the West, it had been virtually bypassed as a land of forests and swamps, of endless winter.

The men behind the new railroad did not intend to change the face of these woods. Poor soils and harsh climate precluded any wave of immigration comparable to what was happening in Minnesota and the Dakota Territory. Instead, they saw the line as a critical augmentation of their businesses —a new and better connection between their thundering flour mills in Minneapolis and eager customers in the East.

Eventually, their new enterprise would also improve access to granaries opening up along the Red River, across the Dakotas, and even in Montana. But for now, the men looked east. They would deliberately route their tracks far from the other major rail arteries that served the seaboard via Chicago. They would cut their route across the emptiest parts of three different states—north and east to a remote border outpost on the rapids of the St. Mary's River. If they could garner any business along the way, so much the better, but their true goal was five hundred miles away—the settlement named Sault Ste. Marie, popularly called "the Soo."

A new railroad would bring year-round service to that sleepy town that for two hundred years had been cut off from the outside world for six months each winter when the Great Lakes froze over. At the border they would join with Canadians to build a bridge across the treacherous river that drained Lake Superior and formed the boundary between the two countries. That bridge would link their rail line with another equally remote line to be built by Canadians. Together, they would create for the burgeoning industries of Minneapolis a link to eastern and overseas markets that would be their own. It would be shorter and faster than any competitor, and it would be free from interference by Wall Street speculators, Chicago monopolists, and, to a large degree, from the U.S. government.

The country to be covered was fearsome. Since the route crossed topography where the watersheds ran north to south, there were literally hundreds of watercourses to be crossed. Each one had carved its path between long shoulders of rock. Gouged by ancient glaciers, the hills between the watersheds were partly lateral moraines and partly the hardest, oldest rock on the planet. In the low pockets lay mosquito-infested bogs. Every rise in the land ran at right angles to the new route, and most of this high ground was linked so that going around it would be difficult. Just to get across Wisconsin, the railroad would have to ford five significant rivers: the St. Croix, Chippewa, Flambeau, Wisconsin, and Menominee. The quantity of necessary bridging and trestles would be enormous. There were few maps and no roads; surveyors and tree cutters would have to pack everything in on their backs and cut their own supply roads.

In addition, the climate was terrible. Winters were the toughest in the country, and the 1880s were particularly harsh. Temperatures sometimes stayed for weeks well below zero. Hard-frozen ground and wind chill created problems for wood-burning steam locomotives. Steel became brittle, water tanks froze. The packing on steam valves shrank and allowed steam to escape, thus cutting the power of a steam engine in half. Hence, track grades needed to be much gentler than usual. Because of snow and cold, there could be little earth-moving or rail-laying during the winter months. Parts of Michigan's Upper Peninsula averaged over three hundred inches of snow a year. Gales coming off Lake Superior frequently dropped two feet of snow in an evening and then blew it into drifts twice as high as a locomotive by morning. Every trace cut had to be designed with such drifting in mind. When the deep snowpack melted in spring, freshets in the south-flowing streams caused frequent ice jams and flash floods. Where there was lumbering, there were log jams.[22] Every bridge and culvert would have to be able to withstand these hazards. Summers brought stifling heat and clouds of insects, and fall came with droughts and forest fires.

Over the entire five hundred miles, only tiny way stations served the four small railroads that carried trappers, miners, and lumberjacks into the woods and lumber and iron ore out. These lines ran north and south—with the grain of the country, rather than against it. Hundreds of lonely miles separated them. Other than trees, there were no materials to aid in the construction, no reinforced concrete or easily accessible ballasting. Although railroad ties and trestle lumber could be obtained locally, steel rails and hardware would have to be brought in across the Great Lakes and then by rail down to each of the isolated points where the new route intersected existing north-south rail lines. In this sparsely populated territory, surveyors, axe men, scrapers and horses to pull them, carpenters to erect buildings from cook shacks to roundhouses, locomotive engineers, firemen and brakemen, cooks, pay clerks, telegraph operators, and a host of laborers and maintenance men would have to be brought in from the outside.

---

22 In a famous jam on the Chippewa in 1869, logs piled up 30 feet high extended upstream for 15 miles. Robert Nesbit, *The History of Wisconsin* (Madison: Wisconsin Historical Society, 1985) 3: 69.

But there were some good things about the route. Once Captain Rich's survey teams actually got into the country, they discovered that it was flatter than anticipated, if they stayed south of the steep country along Lake Superior. Although the rivers there were wider and deeper, flatter land meant gentler grades, fewer rock cuts, and less snow to block winter operations. Also, the forest offered plenty of wood to fuel steam engines and make trestles. In winter, hard-frozen ice would provide a platform for the equipment that drove piles. Because local mine operators and lumbermen were eager to have a railroad, land could be easily obtained. In the village of Rhinelander, for example, a lumber company donated land for generous switching yards and depot facilities. At the Michigan end of the route, a deep bay— the Bay de Noc— extended in from northern Lake Michigan and looked to be a fine docking location for large deep-water vessels. This would be important to shippers serving southern lake ports at Chicago, Cleveland, and Buffalo because the locks and canal built in the 1850s at Sault Ste. Marie were only 12 feet deep. By the 1880s the biggest ore-carrying vessels required much more depth than that. As every shipper knew, the more load a ship carried, the lower the shipping costs. If the new railroad built a pier and loading facility at Bay de Noc, it might be able to attract business from the iron mines along Lake Superior, as well as eastbound flour and westbound coal shipments.

When Captain Rich at last came out of the woods, he had calculated that the railroad could be built for $13,000 per mile—the same cost as the last railroad he had designed for this area, the Wisconsin Central. That road, however, had run north and south—with the ridges, not across them—and was elevated from high water in spring.

Since 1866 Rich had been involved with surveying and engineering railroads. In Wisconsin, he had built and then operated the most difficult northern end of the Wisconsin Central for eight years. As a consultant, he had worked for both the U.S. government and for capitalists from Boston and Chicago who wanted independent evaluations of potential railroad investments. For the Minneapolis and St. Louis (M&StL), he had overseen western extensions of the road beyond Lake Minnetonka as well as south into Iowa and the coal fields beyond Fort Dodge. He had also brought about important improvements all along its route. He had impressed William Washburn with his diligence.

Back in Minneapolis, there was optimism, but little appreciation of the problems to be faced. Many millers had been successful investors in timberlands and sawmills, but few had actually wielded a double-bladed ax in subzero weather. Only two had had any actual experience building railroads.

But this was not their assignment. These men were to raise money for pushing the project forward. At Rich's rate of $13,000 a mile, they would need no less than $6.5 million to get the job done. This was a mountain far larger than anything Rich would confront in the woods.

As the rail line penetrated the forest, small lumber camps and backwoods sawmills along their route might provide some income for operating expenses. But there was no way the prodigious expense could be recouped from these operations. That would not happen—could not happen—until the entire route was complete and the flour trains rumbled uninterrupted to Canada. In the meantime, cash would be needed to buy mountains of construction materials, supplies, and rolling stock for the line. Huge amounts of earth would have to be moved, as rough spots were smoothed, high spots leveled, low spots filled in, and dikes constructed to support tracks across the bogs. For the entire time needed to survey and construct the line—perhaps as long as five years—payrolls would have to be met. If they tried to hurry, more men, material, and money would be needed sooner. No grades could be scraped nor rails laid between December and April.

To attract investors, Minneapolis's millers would have to issue bonds, which could also serve as collateral for loans they took out. Sooner or later, interest would have to be paid on the bonds. If the millers sold stock, dividends would eventually have to be paid. If they delayed too long on either, their reputations, and the road's reputation, would join the scrap pile of over-sold railroad schemes.

In this project there would be no fertile government land to sell or lease out. There would be no wave of would-be farmer immigrants to encourage or agricultural products to ship out. On the projected Soo Line, the land was privately held, and the route went in the opposite direction

Minnesota Historical Society

"President" William Drew Washburn in the 1880s, at the time he was head of the Washburn Mill Company and the Minneapolis and St. Louis Railroad.

from the westward expansion the government encouraged. There would be no help from either state or federal governments in getting this line built. Its investors would be on their own.

The millers and businessmen were aware of these challenges, but they were driven by greater worries—about the future security of their businesses. James J. Hill's new rail link with the Duluth line at Hinckley meant that Minneapolis could lose most of the spring wheat that was beginning to pour out of the Red River Valley. Booming Duluth was building facilities that could load 75,000 barrels of wheat into a ship in an hour and a half. Enlarged locks planned at Sault Ste. Marie would lower shipping times from Duluth to Buffalo to three-and-one-half days. In addition, hostile Chicago railroads made their own transportation costs a large question mark. As eastern customers demanded larger and larger volumes of flour, these customers wanted sales contracts that locked in prices into the future. The slightest alterations in the millers' operating costs—such as an arbitrary rise in their freight rates—could mean the difference between a banner year and a disaster.

For 10 years Minneapolis's millers had wavered about moving ahead. In the meantime, a plethora of new rail mergers and construction had exploded around them— and not a mile of the new lines with rates they could control or predict. Now, a new chance, perhaps the last, was opening up. They knew nothing about running a railroad. Most of them didn't want to. What they needed was somebody to take the lead, someone to whip up investor excitement and with enough experience to see the project through.

And there in front of them was William Washburn—with fire in his eye and experience in building railroads. He had the energy. And he appeared to be fearless. Time after time, he had been humiliated and seemingly destroyed, and here he was back with another wild enthusiasm, an idea that would solve their transportation troubles—forever. William spoke to their every frustration and gave wing to their hopes. He was a miller, just like them. His dream was their dream.

Far from being leveled by being removed from Washburn-Crosby and the Minneapolis and St. Louis road, William was on a roll. In politics, he had just been re-elected to Congress for the third time. At home, he was at work on a spectacular family castle, Fair Oaks— the most opulent mansion that Minneapolis had ever seen. In business—no longer under the protective eye of his departed brother, Cadwallader—William's own mills were doing well. Lumber prices had been high for a year, and William estimated his 1882 production to be 25 million feet, which enabled him to pay off $5,000 in loans to his brother Elihu, and to take on new ones. On top of that, his operations at Anoka were steadily expanding.

Through a provision in Cadwallader's will, William had been reinserted for a third time into the management of Washburn-Crosby milling—this time to represent the family. There he would bedevil manager John Crosby for the nearly five years it would take to settle the estate. When Crosby died in 1887, among the many new managers brought in, the last one, as managing partner, was the modest Philadelphia flour miller James Stroud Bell. Again there was a collision— William was heard calling Bell "a great bullfrog"—and, for the third and final time, William was expelled from his brother's flour company.[23]

William had better luck in a spectacular brush with St. Paul's James J. Hill at the posh watering hole of Lake Minnetonka, and everybody who was anybody in Minneapolis watched it happen. For "rusticators" from the Deep South, Minnetonka had become the equivalent of Bar Harbor, Newport, and Saratoga. William had persuaded the M&StL not only to build a line along the south shore of the lake in competition with Hill's Manitoba line along

---

23   James Gray, *Business Without Boundary, The Story of General Mills* (Minneapolis: University of Minnesota Press, 1954), 45.

the north shore, but also to take a half-interest in the fashionable Lake Park Hotel—in direct competition with Hill's grand Hotel Lafayette, the "Saratoga of the West."[24] To compound the impudence, William sunk $57,000 of his own money into the beautiful *City of St. Louis*, a steamboat to service hotels along the lake. Boasting a capacity of one thousand passengers and the first electrically-lit vessel in the country, it was launched in time for the summer season of 1881 and quickly became a local wonder.[25]

Hill was not one to be upstaged for long. The following summer, he launched an even larger steamboat, *Belle of Minnetonka*, with a capacity of 2,500, enlivening life at the lake for the gentry with fiery races between the two boats. No boilers exploded, but several smoke stacks burned out. Finally, in the spirit of sanity and efficient capitalism, Hill quietly bought Washburn's boat the next season. William, grinning, pocketed the money and went looking for new projects.[26]

Regardless of their feelings about each other, Washburn and Hill walked some similar paths to success. They were close contemporaries— Washburn in Minneapolis, Hill in St. Paul—and although active in a variety of enterprises, they each fixed on building railroads. Both were fearless. Both had big dreams and saw them become reality. Washburn, with eternal optimism, was a promoter who also had an important career in politics. Hill was far the better manager, a harder worker, and he concentrated his attention. In the end, Hill built better. But for a while, as with their steamboats on Minnetonka, they ran a close race.

The two men probably did not like each other much, but neither let personal feelings color their business decisions. As early as 1867, Hill had coveted the business of transporting flour.[27] Washburn several times

---

24 With an eye on the expansion of wheat farms further west, William kept extending his line further to the south and west. By 1881 it had reached Winthrop, 69 miles from Minneapolis.

25 Don L. Hofsommer, *The Tootin' Louie, A History of the Minneapolis and St. Louis Railway* (Minneapolis: University of Minnesota Press, 2005), 28. The steamboat was "painted a glittering white picked out with gold and she looked like a wedding cake, all tiers dripping with white scrollwork." Thelma Jones, *Once Upon a Lake* (Minneapolis: Ross and Haines, 1969), 252.

26 Don L. Hofsommer, *Minneapolis and the Age of Railways* (Minneapolis: University of Minnesota Press, 2005), 93.

27 Wills, *Boosters*, 126.

Minnesota Historical Society

Lake Minnetonka was the site of William Washburn's and James J. Hill's steamboat competition. By 1895, when this picture was taken, both boats belonged to J. J. Hill.

courted Hill as an investor in the Minneapolis Mill Company. Hill was happy to accept Washburn's help in acquiring land for the approaches to the beautiful stone-arch railroad bridge Hill completed at Minneapolis in 1883 (today, one of the city's leading landmarks). Hill even had no objection to the millers' dream of a railroad east, just as long as they stayed out of his burgeoning empire to the west. However, William's new project, the "Soo Line" railroad, would end up being an irritant for Hill over the next 20 years.

Since the end of the Civil War, the most dramatic American railroad building had taken place far to the west of Wisconsin. To the Wall Street crowd, the thundering flour mills at Minneapolis were an unexpected miracle in what had seemed just the other day to have been country only inhabited by Indians. Burned by the Jay Cooke collapse in 1873, New York money men were slow to realize that as customers from Boston to Bucharest clamored for Minnesota flour, dependable year-round transportation was the highest priority for both millers and farmers. So the Minnesota men would have to get their railroad project off the ground by themselves.

Across the Northwest in the early 1880s, the long economic doldrums appeared to be breaking up. The flame for an independent railroad lit by Israel Washburn, Jr., 10 years earlier that had been smoldering amid economic stagnation, rate wars, political scandal, bankruptcies, and takeovers, finally burst into open fire—with William Washburn as the catalyst.

One September day in 1883, Washburn called on his old colleague Henry Welles, who agreed with him that the Sault St. Marie route was attractive and that economic times were good for getting local investment support.[28] This was confirmed the very next day, when they called together a large group of influential business friends in Washburn's Minneapolis office. The men subsequently invited to membership on the new company's board formed a cross-section of the city's power elite representing the major milling companies, the biggest banks, and a scattering of other leading businessmen—every one of whom stood to benefit from a shorter rail route to the east. Henry Welles and W. W. Eastman, the oldest members, had interests in everything from lumber to hotels. Eastman's Cataract Mill had been William's first tenant on the canal. While Cadwallader Washburn had just died, one of his most trusted lieutenants from Washburn-Crosby, Charles J. Martin, was there. Charles A. Pillsbury himself was in the group, to be replaced by his uncle, John S. after the first year. Clinton Morrison, son of William's cousin Dorilus Morrison, represented harvesting-machinery, a woolen mill, and a bank. He would be replaced the first year by C. H. Pettit, lumberman and owner of the Pettit Mill. Capt. John Martin was a former steamboat captain and owner of the Northwestern Mill. Also there was J. K. Sidle of the First National Bank of Minneapolis, who also owned a mill, and who provided a room at his bank for the new board's meetings. George Newell, one of William's early partners, and Anthony

---

28   There is no specific information about the date Washburn met with Welles, or when Washburn got the first survey money or sent out the first survey teams. Reminiscences suggest that it was between August and late September. Documented dates are September 29, when the first corporation was approved in Wisconsin, and October 25, when Captain Rich was hired.

Kelley were the leading wholesale grocers in town. Younger Charles Loring would soon become the most respected miller in town. Rounding out the group was Thomas Lowry, William's partner in the street railway project, and William Hale, who had managed W. D. Washburn Co. for William, had risen to be a partner in the Minneapolis Milling Company, and was now secretary of John Martin's Northwest Milling Company.

Each man had been in the city for years. Each had probably listened to William's brother Israel 10 years before. Each was in the new venture for the long haul. William had the experience, the enthusiasm, and the contacts to get the project started. These men would see to it that the financing would be taken care of—at least at the beginning.

To William's credit the galaxy of the city's leaders stepped aboard his train without hesitation. His enthusiasms were so infectious that on the same day he pulled in pledges totaling $10,000 for a preliminary survey for the new railroad. Within weeks, he had much more.

Washburn immediately sent four survey parties out to begin the search for a specific route through the wilderness. The next month he took his board east to Hudson, Wisconsin, to sign the Wisconsin incorporation papers and to have their first board meeting. Without a grumble, the men pledged to buy a million dollars in stock for the new road. The incorporation papers were approved in Madison on September 29, 1883. The Minneapolis, Sault Ste. Marie and Atlantic Railroad was in business.[29]

Back in Minneapolis, the group convened to elect William as president, John S. Pillsbury (Charles' uncle) as vice president, and C. H. Pettit as treasurer. Captain Rich was appointed chief engineer in charge of engineering and construction. The "Soo Line" as it became known, was underway, and William's next great adventure had begun.

A few days later, William summoned Captain Rich to his office in Minneapolis. The men made an interesting contrast. Washburn—tall, slender, and impeccably turned out—was older, better educated, and articulate. He preached and he danced. Captain Rich— shorter and scruffier and looking more like a wrestler—expressed himself like the workman he

---

29   The line was first incorporated in 1883 as the Minneapolis, Sault Ste. Marie and Atlantic Railroad. The nickname "Soo Line" became official in 1961.

Soo Line Historical and Technical Society
Captain Rich, Washburn's able surveyor, construction supervisor, and general manager, about 1895.

was. After a few weeks in the woods, his beard looked self-trimmed with a dull pair of scissors. Washburn was well-spoken, reserved, but with a flair for persuading. Rich could be humorous, had a more common touch, and spoke as he stood, bluntly, with feet apart. Washburn's audience would get well-shaped, logical, and compelling images of things that were to come and might be. Rich's audience would get an unvarnished statement of things as they were. Over the next five years, the two men would not interfere with each others' kingdoms but do great things together.

Washburn, familiar with Rich's past work, wanted him badly to head the Soo project. On the back of the employment contract they signed that day—October 25, 1883—in his own hand, Washburn personally guaranteed Rich a year's salary regardless of whether or not the work got done. From that point on, the captain would superintend, and Washburn would raise the money to pay.

William first asked the engineer to review the work of the four survey parties already dispatched in Wisconsin, look over the country, and estimate the actual construction costs. After tramping almost 180 miles, the imperturbable Captain Rich returned with his estimate of $13,000 per mile. By this time, Washburn was deep into negotiations for land in Minneapolis for Soo Line shops, freight yards, and roundhouses. Subscriptions for stock in the new line rolled in. It was the kind of action that Washburn loved.

Washburn was looking west as well as east. Long before a foot of track was laid, even before the company had been formed— and just two days after the huge September 1883 celebration in St. Paul to honor the completion of the Northern Pacific to Tacoma, Washington—William had gone to North Dakota with tycoon James J. Hill and Henry Villard, accompanied by newspaperman Joseph Pulitzer and former Minnesota governor Henry H. Sibley, Chicago merchant Marshall Field, and Indian leader Sitting Bull, to help ex-President Ulysses Grant lay the cornerstone for the new territorial capitol in Bismarck. Hill must have wondered about Washburn's interest in North Dakota, although the ceremony in the prairie town went off without a hitch.

Unlike many early railroads, the Soo Line was not a scheme to make a quick buck by selling railroad land and then getting out. There would be no construction scandal comparable to Crédit Mobilier, either. The Soo's contractors would be local and would earn every penny that they were paid. There were no government lands to promote, hence no land speculation and no inflated prices. There would be no over-promoted sale of stock to the public, or stock watering, or secret reorganizations. The owners were looking for security for their milling businesses, and this railroad would help achieve that security. Its construction would be clean, its operations transparent.

William hoped that the initial surge of cash would be enough to get the surveys done and fund maybe two years of construction. Nobody knew exactly how long the entire job would take, but all knew that they would not get a penny of real benefit until the line was usable all the way to its end—and until the Canadians had finished their construction to meet it.

Racing to beat the advancing winter, Rich visited and redirected each of the four advance survey teams as his budget and their early information seemed to dictate. There were many questions to be answered, and Captain Rich needed to see each obstacle for himself. The Chippewa River, and its attendant hills, represented the first big challenge. Rich wasted no time. After a flying visit to the crew surveying the route between Minneapolis and the first big river, the St. Croix, he headed on foot east into the woods from Cameron, Wisconsin, a small settlement established two years earlier by the northbound Omaha railroad.

Washburn's board was not a group of absentee investors. One of them, John Martin, a Yankee lumberman who also was called "Captain" in deference to his experience piloting steamboats, joined Captain Rich in the woods to scout the Chippewa River from south to north. On November 11, they met the second survey party under a T. A. Lang that had been trying to find a more southerly line along the valley of the Jump

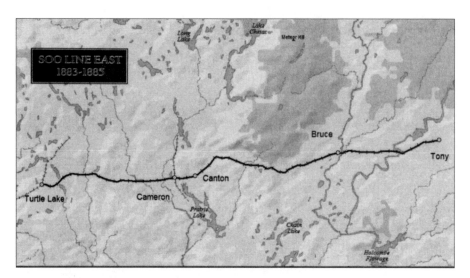

Early Soo Line surveying and construction across the Wisconsin woods took place between 1883 and 1885 from Turtle Lake to Tony. Between 1886 and 1887, the Soo completed the link back to Minneapolis over the canyon of the St. Croix River at Osceola.

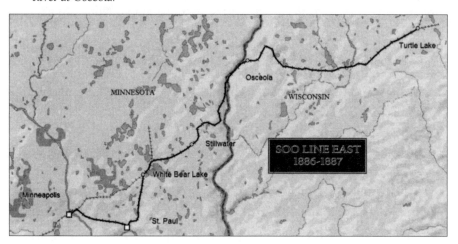

River, another Chippewa tributary. The country was extremely broken up, and the expense looked formidable. Both Rich and Martin believed that the potential for lumber business made a more northerly route desirable.

Rich took great pains to explore all the possibilities personally. At one point, his surveyors under Warren Dunbar had actually completed three separate survey lines extending for many miles east of Cameron. Finally, working in two feet of snow, Dunbar found a route along the Thornapple River that he thought could be accomplished at a grade of 0.8 percent, although it would require massive earthmoving. Rich finally agreed, sending Dunbar west from the Chippewa at the end of January to locate the route that would end at the present station of Canton.

Racing winter, Rich sent the Lang party back to Cameron to find a line west to Turtle Lake. After much frustration, Lang finally found a route. Lang then moved east to establish a line to the Flambeau River, where again several crossings were explored and rejected, before a final one was selected. Rich himself, still with his guide, headed east toward Rhinelander and the formidable Wisconsin River. There, on November 16, he found the third survey party of 21 packers and surveyors led by E.M. Spaulding. To both Spaulding and Rich, the swampy county looked extremely difficult, with "very heavy earthwork" required if the route was to stay above water. It would be a year before a crossing over the Wisconsin would be determined from five possibilities along a 20-mile stretch.

As Rich had feared, the surveys proved much more expensive than other railroad survey jobs. To save money, Rich disbanded the Spaulding party and directed their leader with a smaller group to look for a route further to the north. This party tracked back from the Flambeau to the north and west but found nothing suitable and disbanded.

Captain Rich and his guide continued to the east, reaching the fourth survey party, a group of 19 men and packers under G. M. Willis that was exploring a route toward Michigan north and east of Rhinelander, on the other side of the Wisconsin River headwaters. Again, Rich decided to cut the party down. He sent just five of them on a huge circle north to the Detroit, Mackinac and Marquette Railroad near Lake Superior, then south again across the Upper Peninsula to the shore of Lake Michigan, where the millers had their eye on a possible site for a port, and then westerly again toward Iron Mountain, where the final large river, the Menominee, would have to be crossed. Ominously, temperatures hit minus 47 degrees F. that winter along his route, and Willis found the snow so deep that he could not finish his job until the following winter.[30]

While Rich was laboring to the east, his bosses were endeavoring to buy some time before being forced to invest big money at the western end of the new line. William had emerged from his removal from the M&StP presidency with a seat on the Omaha board, and in January 1884, he cut a temporary deal to use the Omaha line for its first 60 miles out of Minneapolis, including the bridge across the St. Croix River canyon into Wisconsin. The Soo line would start where the Omaha turned north, at Turtle Lake, Wisconsin. Everyone agreed that construction should start at the westernmost end of the route. The preliminary surveys were complete to the east, and Rich's winter crews had determined the route.

In line with Rich's telegrams, Washburn began to place orders for construction materials. He also placed the order with an experienced Minneapolis contractor to prepare the surface and lay the track for the first 60 miles from Turtle Lake eastward. When another economic slowdown hit in April, the plan was modified to go as far as the Chippewa and no further that year, some 46 miles.

Since the Omaha line crossed Rich's proposed route at the mid-point of the planned first year's construction at Cameron, Rich suggested that construction headquarters the first year be set up there, allowing crews to work both eastward and westward at the same time. Sleepy Cameron, deep in the Wisconsin woods, had never seen anything like what descended on it in April 1884 when the first shovelful of dirt was turned for a marshalling yard and for space to pile up mountains of ties that began to arrive from the north woods. Since Rich planned to use up to 3,000 ties for every mile of track and siding he laid, Washburn had ordered 160,000 ties, each seven inches square, to be stacked around Cameron. Further mountains of 56-lb. Pennsylvania steel rails also began to arrive on the Omaha line from the Lake Superior port of Washburn,

---

30   Karl Bohnak, *So Cold a Sky, Upper Michigan Weather Stories* (Negaunee, Michigan: Cold Sky Publishing, 2006), 127.

Wisconsin (named after Cadwallader, the state's former governor) Fishplates and bolts to hold the rails together, plus many of their workers, came up the Omaha line from Chicago.

The contractor, Henry and Balch, threw up warehouses and an office right across the street from the depot. Omaha agent Richard A. Burton suddenly found himself busy with telegrams and directing incoming and outgoing supply trains. Outside his office, the land was graded, ties were put down, and rails were laid, followed, as purse strings allowed, by surfacing and ballasting. Right behind the new sidings came rolling stock for the new line—eventually 40 flat cars and, in late June, the first engine. Amid huge excitement Locomotive No. 1—built by the Rhode Island Locomotive Works—arrived in pieces for assembly. A second engine arrived two weeks later. Both locomotives were wood burners, 4-4-0s, each with its distinctive diamond-shaped funnel and four huge 56-inch driving wheels. Each engine weighed about 42 tons.[31] The second engine was taken to Turtle Lake, where, by the next winter, a three-stall roundhouse was built.

The man they put in charge of the roundhouse, who had been driving the second engine, was a young jack-of-all-trades from Vermont named Daniel Willard. Over the next 16 years, he would rise within the Soo Line to trainmaster, then division superintendent, and eventually president of the mighty Baltimore and Ohio Railroad, where his assistant for more than 20 years was William Drew Washburn's son, Edwin.

Willard later recorded memories of the early days on the Soo. After being laid off from his job as locomotive engineer in Indiana, he had arrived at Cameron with one other man. They had boarded the Omaha line in Chicago, ridden all night, and been deposited at daybreak in what looked like the middle of nowhere. His companion quit after just two weeks, "swearing by all that was holy that he never wanted to see northern Wisconsin again."[32] This might have been because they had to sleep on

---

31   Although a source of great pride at the time, these engines were tiny in comparison with those that followed. So was the length of the trains they could haul and their 56-lb rail (compared to the 136-lb rail of later years).

32   Edward Hungerford, *Daniel Willard Rides the Line* (New York: G. P. Putnam's Sons, 1938), 76.

Soo Line Historical and Technical Society

The Soo Line's just-arrived wood-burning Engine #2 with its crew on the newly-laid track at Cameron, Wisconsin. The engineer in the cab could be Daniel Willard, who became head of the mighty Chesapeake and Ohio Railroad. Note the absence of any ballast between or under the new ties.

the floor of a box car. It might have been because food and opportunities to take baths were minimal. It might have been because, after two weeks, the entire enterprise consisted of just one engine, a half-mile of track, and a half-dozen cars like the one they were sleeping in. But probably it was because of Cameron's isolation. For anyone used to city life, northern Wisconsin in 1884 was close to the end of the world.

Willard stuck it out, however. He enjoyed opportunities to hunt and fish in the forests and ponds around him. Originally hired as brakeman on the construction train, he was promoted to conductor as the track lengthened out from Cameron. When the second engine was ready, they permitted him to get it in Eau Claire, and he was at the controls when it chuffed into the clearing at Cameron and onto the new line's tracks.

Nobody had more fun that year, however, than William Washburn. Willard remembered William in his usual high collar and business suit, planted on a soap box on a flatcar being pushed in front of an engine through the forest to examine progress on the line. William even drove the engine himself. Willard was much too discreet to mention how fast the boss went but the picture of the little engine bucketing along the primitive track through the woods can be imagined—along with the gleam in the boss's eye.

Construction in both directions out from Cameron went quickly that first year, and the new road was complete from Turtle Lake to the last station short of the Chippewa in August. They named the latter place Bruce. To get there, Rich later reported that it had taken more than 800,000 cubic yards of earthwork, but he had kept the grade to 0.8 percent for 46 miles, an engineering triumph.

As Rich pointed out in his 1885 report, construction also included other items besides track. Locomotives were driven by steam, and that meant they needed frequent water. The railroad needed to build water towers with stone foundations and steam pumps in frost-proof houses every 25 or 30 miles along the route. At least one building was built at each watering station, a depot with waiting rooms, storage space for small freight, and offices, all painted. Thirty cedar telegraph poles per mile, each 25 feet long and set five feet into the ground, had to be installed. And since the line was single track, there had to be frequent sidings so that trains could get around one another.

All this activity ate through the millers' initial investment capital very quickly, and despite every economy, the bottom of the barrel was soon in sight. When another national recession tightened up the money supply, the millers again pulled in their horns. William's board rejected the idea of floating an issue of stock, although an enormous amount of work still had to be done. The Chippewa had yet to be crossed, plus hundreds of miles of rough country beyond that. A rumor circulated that the board had approached the Omaha road about taking over but been turned down.

In the face of this anxiety, William, ever the promoter, decided to celebrate. In November, he organized a special train of four cars—three new coaches and a new baggage car—to carry 75 stockholders, friends, and reporters to show off the track from Turtle Lake to Bruce. When the group saw the trackless wilderness first hand, some of them must have shuddered.

The mood was probably not improved by the political news that day. The presidential election of 1884 had just been held, and the final result did not come in until the train of reluctant adventurers had disappeared into the woods beyond the last telegraph line at Cameron. When they returned to Cameron that afternoon, it fell to the unfortunate telegrapher to tell them the bad news that Democrat Grover Cleveland had won—the first Republican presidential loss since before the Civil War. Telegrapher Burton never forgot the resulting uproar that afternoon.

William's grand effort at public relations ended on a most gloomy note. Plans for 1885 were scaled back, and Rich was authorized to plan for only 25 miles. Soo stockholders were assessed an additional 15 percent, which most paid. The future looked grim.

The miles constructed in 1885 were hard ones. Crews waited until the Chippewa had frozen, then raced through the depth of the winter of 1884–85, using the ice to support their equipment and driving piles for the new bridge before the spring melt. Some piles were 65 feet long. Fortunately, the ice lasted just long enough that winter and the men got the job done. With the coming of spring, heavy rains loosened the rocky hillsides and inundated low-lying swamps that seemed to have no bottom even before they were flooded. With crews reduced, there was as much bridge and trestle building as there was laying of rail that year. But by the end of the season, the railroad had not only crossed the Chippewa, but also the neighboring Flambeau River. Work for 1885 stopped beyond the Flambeau at a spot a few miles over the divide called Main Creek (now Tony). They were on the down slope into the drainage of the Wisconsin River. They were also out of money.

Back in Minneapolis, despite the gloomy economic picture, Washburn succeeded in contracting for joint use of the Minneapolis terminal of the Northern Pacific Railroad, as well as in acquiring 160 acres of land in northeastern Minneapolis for shops, a roundhouse, and a rail yard. He created two new railroad corporations registered in Minnesota. One of them was to construct the 75 miles from Minneapolis to Turtle Lake—including its own swing drawbridge over the St. Croix River at Osceola. The other, immodestly called the

Wisconsin Historical Society

This winter view of the lower Flambeau River in Wisconsin in 1900 evidences the rough country to be tamed for the Soo Line.

Minneapolis and Pacific Railroad, was for a new feeder system onto the prairies west of Minneapolis. The fact that this would compete directly with James J. Hill's Manitoba road bothered William not a whit. As on Lake Minnetonka, Washburn did not fear Hill. He didn't want to depend on Hill's line to get his grain in to the mills, any more than he wanted to depend on the Chicago manipulators to get his flour out of the mills.

With his executive committee behind him, Washburn turned to the idea of building a port on northern Lake Michigan. A sheltered, deep-water spot just off their proposed route at Saunders Point on the Little

Bay de Noc, seemed promising, and in June 1885, Washburn pulled Captain Rich out of the woods, hired a steam tug, and with his executive committee made a personal reconnoiter from Escanaba along Lake Michigan's shore all the way to Manistique.

Lake Michigan had a big advantage over Lake Superior for shipping. The limited size of the Sault Ste. Marie canal and the shallowness of the St. Mary's River below it meant that deep-draft ships could not get in or out of Lake Superior. They could, however, transit Lakes Michigan, Huron, the Detroit River, and Lake Erie. Heavyweight vessels could, in season, carry large loads directly from Little Bay de Noc to Buffalo, or Cleveland, or Chicago. Thanks to the new railroad, these loads could be flour or wheat from Minneapolis or the plains, as well as iron ore from the fledgling mines in Upper Michigan at Iron Mountain and Negaunee beyond.

The board and Captain Rich liked what they saw at Saunders Point. A key nudge had been supplied in April by lumber operator Charles J. L. Meyer in Fond du Lac. He had large holdings in timberlands between Rhinelander and the Menominee River and beyond it in the forest around Hermansville, Michigan. Meyer was enthusiastic about a potential route that went considerably south of where Rich's surveyors had originally explored around Florence—and much closer to Lake Michigan. Meyer said it was shorter than the more northerly route, with easier grades, less expensive construction, and less snow. Furthermore, it went right through the heart of a magnificent pinery—two to three billion feet of highly marketable timber. Because much of the watershed of the Menominee was too shallow to float logs, lumbermen here would have to ship out by rail—which meant immediate business for the railroad. In addition, there was so much hardwood in the forest that Meyer himself was considering building a hardwood factory on the new line, if Washburn would redirect it that way.[33] The iron mines to the north, Meyer went on to say, were already under contract to other railroads and harbors in the north, so there would be legal difficulties in getting them to break those contracts. Only the southern route promised a litigation-free port. He wrote Washburn a 20-page

---

[33] He did, and the company is still there today.

presentation of the idea and capped it off by offering to pay for a fresh survey of the area he had in mind.

There is no listener more receptive to a good sales pitch than a salesman himself, and William Washburn made a side trip to see Meyer at Hermansville during his 1885 expedition to Bay de Noc. He was impressed enough to attach Meyer's entire letter in his 1885 Annual Report to shareholders. Washburn also got confirmation that lumbermen working the upper Wisconsin and Tomahawk Rivers would welcome the arrival of an east-west line downstream from where they were cutting. William's directors took Meyer up on his offer, and Rich made sure that his surveyor Willis had a good look at the country downstream on the Menominee River from Florence, where the first surveys had been done. At Bay de Noc, a contract was drawn up to purchase 160 acres for a rail yard at Saunders Point and to obtain a half interest in another 800 acres for a town site adjacent to it. Plans were also made to start work on a large pier there.

However, even after all this, by the time 1886 dawned, the Soo Line was still three-quarters un-built, and its coffers were nearly dry. It was time for William to pull another rabbit out of the hat. He succeeded in spectacular fashion—not in New York or Philadelphia, but in Montreal.

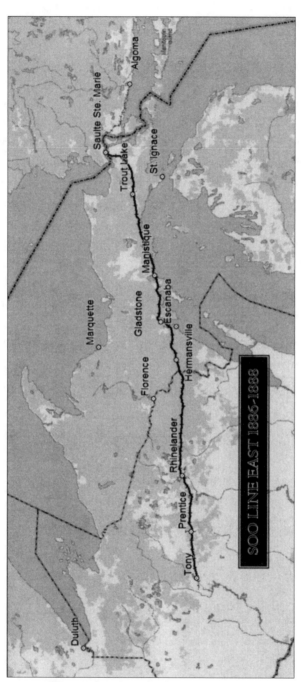

British and Canadian money made possible the last long link of the Soo Line eastward through the wilderness of northern Wisconsin and Michigan's Upper Peninsula.

5

Triumph at the Soo
1886–1888

For two days it had been snowing. The howling winds off the frozen lake had created huge drifts on the lee side of every building, telegraph pole, and piece of equipment around the new station. The depot building itself had a drift to its eves. Fortunately for the figures huddled there, the platform side of the station faced the lake and was blown almost bare. Bundled up though they were, the wind still cut like a knife and watered their eyes. Some faced to the west, some faced to the east. All listened for the distant screech of a train whistle—from either direction. Finally, faintly, through the clouds of blowing snow, they heard it. Through frozen lips and cheeks, they cheered. Men danced, hugged their ladies, and pounded each other on the back. This day, January 5, 1888, was without a doubt the greatest day in the history of Sault Ste. Marie, Michigan.

At the end of the 1885 season, Soo Line construction deep in the northern forest finally sputtered to a halt. Crews had completed only a little over 25 miles that year. Behind them, they had built a 120-mile hole through the woods from nowhere to nowhere. They still had 300 miles more to go. On the other side of the national boundary, the Canadians had yet to start their work. Despite William Washburn's most ardent efforts to raise capital, Minneapolis's millers had poured into the project about as much money as they could. Even though Captain Rich, through taking lumber supplies into the woods and carrying logs out, miraculously made more money on the new line than it cost to run it, it was obvious that much more money would be needed than the millers could put up themselves. In May 1885, the board had elected to mortgage everything built so far. They raised another two million dollars this way, which enabled them to incorporate in Michigan and start work there. This was the final move that they could make. They were tapped out. There was no more money—in Minneapolis, anyway.

The project's future was now entirely in the hands of William Drew Washburn. He might have alienated most of the managers he had ever tried to work with, but, right now, he was the millers' last hope for an independent Soo Line. If anyone could save this project, it had to be him.

As Washburn packed his bag once again to head east in search of financing, he might have considered visiting the great financial centers in New York and Philadelphia. Both had helped him in the past—Philadelphians with the flour business and with the Minneapolis and St. Louis Railroad. New Yorkers had helped keep the latter out of the hands of the Chicago pool and had enabled his brother Cadwallader Washburn to bow out of the railroad business.

But William couldn't forget the humiliations brought on by the fall of Jay Cooke's bank back in 1873, by the Philadelphian James Bell who was about to take over the management of Washburn Crosby milling, and by the further humiliation of having Cadwallader's sell-out in New York ultimately force William's own removal from the presidency of the M&StL. So, when he got east, William kept on going—to Montreal, where he had an appointment with Richard T. Angus. Full of his usual confidence and enthusiasm, Washburn bearded the lion in his den—the headquarters of the Bank of Montreal, the biggest bank in Canada. (From there, he would go on to London to talk with the British.)

Geographically, Canada's sparsely populated midsection, until in 1871 it changed from Rupert's Land to the provinces of Manitoba, Saskatchewan and Alberta, was isolated from the rest of Canada by the thousand miles of Cambrian Shield barrier to the east and the equally wide Rocky Mountain barrier to the west. Its economy was the Hudson's Bay Company, which received most of its supplies through Minnesota. The traffic was so heavy that the company maintained an agent and a busy office in St. Paul.

Canadian James J. Hill had gotten his start as a freight agent in St. Paul, and his Red River Transportation Co. ran supplies across Minnesota to Hudson's Bay Company headquarters at Fort Gary

(Winnipeg). Americans living south of the border had long been used to the screeching axles of ox-drawn, wooden-wheeled Pembina carts heading for what became Manitoba. The actual border was unmarked and little regarded. When Hill, and later William Van Horne, threw the first Canadian Pacific railroad tracks across Manitoba, they hired a Minnesota contractor to build the line.

Wikipedia, Canadian Pacific Archives

Washburn's railroad rivals, partners, and saviors: James J. Hill, founder of the Great Northern Railroad, William C. Van Horne, boss of the Canadian Pacific Railroad, and Richard B. Angus, head of the Bank of Montreal.

The volume of Canadian commerce through Minnesota was heavy enough that the president of the Bank of Montreal, a canny Scot named George Steven, sent his closest bank associate, Richard Angus, to operate the office in St. Paul for most of five years. Thanks to their close financial involvement with Hill's Manitoba line in the 1870s, there was little about Minnesota flour milling or railroading that Steven and Angus didn't know.

Canadian politics in the person of Prime Minister John A. MacDonald (who hated Americans) tore practical considerations asunder, however. MacDonald's single-minded drive to keep the Canadian Pacific (CP) an all-Canada line and route it through every barrier north of Lake Superior seemed so impractical that Hill resigned from the CP to concentrate on his own St. Paul, Minneapolis, and Manitoba line that he operated from St. Paul. This resulted in Cornelius Van Horne's ascension to leadership of the Canadian Pacific. Hill's American protégé, Van Horne became Hill's equal in muscling railroads through impossible odds. Steven and Angus, the two Montreal bankers, aided by former Hudson's Bay head Donald Smith, managed to retain their places in both the Manitoba and CP railroad camps.

Although there were only about 3.5 million people living in Canada, the Bank of Montreal had a charter to operate across the entire continent. Long the backer of the Hudson's Bay Company, the bank had resources equal to financial giants in New York and Philadelphia. The bank had already funded thousands of miles of railroad in eastern Canada so it knew the business. In addition, Steven, Smith, and Angus had made a great deal of money out of Hill's Manitoba line by 1880—the year that Angus succeeded Stephen as General Manager of the bank. By 1885, their spectacular CP project, although it had nearly killed them, was complete to the Pacific. The exhausted Stephen would receive a knighthood and then retire to a castle in Scotland.

As Van Horne rammed the Canadian Pacific across the shield country to Manitoba and then the formidable mountains and gorges to the Pacific, Hill slowly spread his Great Northern empire across the Dakota plains to the south. It was a chaotic time for the railroads. States were generous with land grants, and rival entrepreneurs gobbled each other up in mad scrambles. New lines sprouted up in all directions—on paper. There was no central oversight and no long-term security for anyone. Today's ally could be tomorrow's enemy. Van Horne, a pirate in his own right, realized his vulnerability to attack from the south as well as his need for an alternative route if anything ever happened to cut his fragile CP line across the desolate north. In addition, politicians in Ottawa began to realize that the CP was the only thing linking the new country together, and it was as vulnerable to weather or American adventurism as the rest of the country.

Van Horne's bankers agreed with him. Security, in the form of a stake in another east-west route south of Lake Superior, was desirable for the CP. They were also dazzled by the prospects for freight revenue in Canada coming from the booming flour mills in Minneapolis.

In 1883, Washburn's Minneapolis and St. Louis (M&StL) Railroad extending south across Iowa had reached a booming settlement called Coaltown, where nine major coal companies were digging. There the railroad erected a roundhouse, station, and terminal headquarters, plus rail yards and spur lines out to the various diggings. Long, heavy trains of coal rumbled across the fields back to Albert Lea and the Twin Cities to heat homes. The availability of coal also made it easier for the railroads to replace old wood-burning locomotives. Washburn, still on the M&StL's board, arranged to have Coaltown renamed "Angus." This was a tip of the hat to the Canadian banker who had made himself useful in railroading and flour milling in the Upper Mississippi valley, a man William had every intention of seeing again.

Following his trip to Montreal and London in 1886, Washburn returned to Minneapolis looking more confident. There followed a flurry of new activity. In December he and Captain Rich went to Rhinelander, beyond the Wisconsin River, where a predecessor of the Chicago and Northwestern had built a line north and south. There they cut deals with local officials for rights-of-way east and west through town and for space for a roundhouse and a yard. Then they went south to Milwaukee to contract with the Wisconsin Central for terminal facilities. Upon his return to Minneapolis, Washburn announced that his road would be pushed through to Rhinelander the following season. Large contracts were let for clearing a right-of-way, obtaining bridge timber, setting pilings, and stocking railroad ties. The size of the orders indicated to observers that Washburn had something more that his usual bravado in his pocket.

On February 4, 1886—a red-letter day for the Minneapolis, Sault Ste. Marie and Atlantic Railroad—Washburn signed a contract with the Bank of Montreal. It confirmed that the company had issued First Mortgage bonds totaling $1.5 million and that the Bank of Montreal had approved a loan of $750,000 with these bonds as security. Then the news got better. Additional mortgage bonds were issued, and with them as security, London banks agreed to loan $9,000,000 more. Finally, as proof that Angus and Stephen were still closely connected with the CP, it was announced in Canada that the CP would complete an 80-mile branch from its line at Algoma, Ontario, to Sault Ste. Marie.

There was now no doubt. Washburn had pulled another rabbit out of the hat. Minneapolis millers would be able to finish their railroad.

In 1886 construction exploded all along the new line. As many as 7,000 men may have been employed by the railroad's contractors that season. But in many ways, the country to be crossed was the worst yet. The Wisconsin was a big river, and the country beyond it was full of rock ledges, huge boulders, and the same deep swamps encountered before. Still without topographic maps or aerial surveys, Captain Rich and his surveyors literally spent weeks looking for a river crossing with the best approaches. They tramped a swath 20 miles up and down both sides and more than a mile inland. When they finally decided where the crossing would be, they had carefully surveyed five different possibilities, each one with vastly different approach routes.

Now, with finances suddenly assured and Washburn breathing impatience to his rear, Captain Rich urged contractors to "crowd the work as fast as possible,"[34] which they did with some innovative strategies. To clear the forest, a line of shanties was built every half mile. Four men hiked to each hut, and teams of two cleared everything for a quarter mile in each direction along the route. They also chopped out a rough track, so that horses and wagons could get to them with supplies. Amid black flies and mosquitoes, woodchips flew and the whole right-of-way took shape at the same time. The result was that horse-powered scraping and leveling teams could start work on the biggest obstacles simultaneously. Every obstacle was attacked by an army, it seemed.

By the end of the 1886 season, not only had the road been completed 70 miles beyond the Wisconsin River into Rhinelander, but work was also under way back in Minnesota, between Minneapolis and Turtle Lake. This included a fresh route via Osceola that went down to, across, and up the other side of the 250-foot-deep canyon of the St. Croix River.

In addition, and to J.J. Hill's considerable displeasure, Washburn's crews were also tearing across western Minnesota between two of Hill's lines and actually in sight of one of them for nearly 25 miles. Hill was particularly upset that two of his board members, bankers Angus and Stephen, were helping pay for the intruder. When confronted, the Canadians claimed ignorance and backed and filled, but in the end they retained their large interest in both lines. The fault was probably Washburn's for in neglecting to tell his Montreal saviors that he also intended to push westward into the Dakotas. He was still angry at Hill for building his Hinckley link in 1871 that diverted grain business from Minneapolis to Duluth.

The rivalry between Washburn and Hill found its way down to the ground level. In 1886, one of William's construction crews and one of

---

34 James Lydon, "History of the Soo Line," 9, in Minnesota Historical Library, St. Paul, Minnesota.

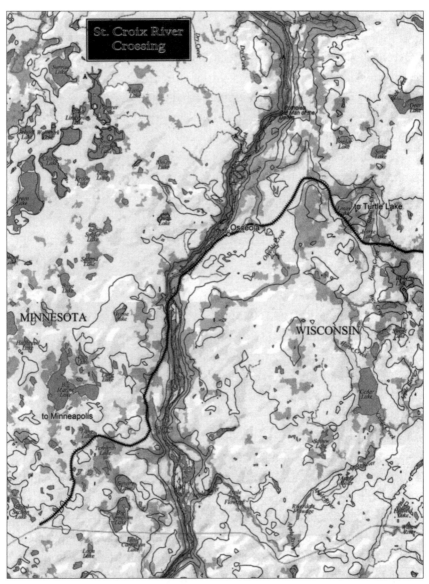

Building the Soo Line across the St. Croix River at Osceola, Wisconsin, required carving a five-mile approach down the 250-foot-deep canyon on each side of the river. River traffic meant construction of a swing bridge, still in use today.

Hill's Manitoba crews—probably two hundred men in all—got into a huge brawl around the county court house in tiny Elbow Lake, Minnesota. Peace was only restored after the local saloon was shut down by the sheriff and its inventory of liquor removed to another town.[35]

A more serious confrontation occurred later at Hankinson, on the Dakota prairie, where Washburn's route crossed a Manitoba route. One evening Hill's crews laid some track along Washburn's grade. Even though title to the land was disputed, this was a direct challenge by one corporation to another. Superintendent Fred Underwood would not let it go without a response. He mounted an armed force and went to the site, but the group arrived after Hill's men had quit for the day. Underwood then commandeered a farmer's horse and overturned a quarter-mile of Hill's track into a ditch. Local sheriffs had to be called in to keep the peace. The contretemps was eventually settled by the lawyers.[36] (Hill admired Underwood's spunk and later helped him get the top job at the Erie Railroad.)

On December 20, 1886, Washburn's western railroad reached beyond the Bois de Sioux River at Lidgerwood, North Dakota. By 1893, with Van Horne pulling strings behind the scenes, it would reach across the entire state to the Canadian border at Portal, thus providing Minneapolis with its second link to the CP line and the far west. Hill could only watch and wait.

Now that William's railroad seemed to have a chance of completion, some big dogs from the South and East moved to get in on the action in Upper Michigan. The contest came over the construction of the bridge across the St. Mary's River at Sault Ste. Marie. To get this international bridge built, Washburn and the Minneapolis millers suddenly faced four rival forces. Every one of them was ready to play hardball.

The first group was headed by James McMillan, leader of a Detroit and New York syndicate that had been buying up small lumber and iron ore roads across the Upper Peninsula to form the Duluth, South Shore and Atlantic Railroad (DSS&A). Having already completed a line from Marquette on Lake Superior to St. Ignace at the Mackinac Straits, this

---

35 Reported in the *Grant County Herald*, October 21, 1886, and the *Fergus Falls Daily Journal*, October 14, 1886.

36 Hard-driving Fred Underwood described this confrontation in a newspaper interview, in *Minneapolis Journal*, November 24, 1928.

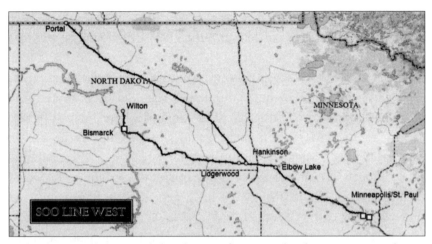

At the same time as it extended to the east of Minneapolis, the Soo Line was also thrown westward. It provided a new shipping route for wheat from the Dakotas and, ultimately, a link with the Canadian Pacific at Portal, North Dakota.

group had the foresight to obtain from Congress the original charter and permit to build the bridge at Sault Ste. Marie. They had just successfully completed a profitable turn-over of the Nickel Plate Line in Ohio and hoped to do the same again with this venture. Their intent was to give fast-growing Duluth the same non-Chicago, year-round rail service that William's group was aiming to achieve for Minneapolis.

The second rival force was the Canadian Pacific, led by the formidable George Steven, Donald Smith, and William Van Horne. Besides having the tightest of relationships with the Canadian government, this group had a superb record in Canada, excellent financing from both Montreal and England, and the inside track on getting things done on the Canadian side of the bridge. Their crews were already building the connection from Algoma to the Canadian side of Sault Ste. Marie.

The third force interested in development was the Grand Trunk Railroad, the predominant railroad in eastern Canada, which, like the CP, had a charter to build to the Sault on the Canadian side. This group had just achieved its own line across central Michigan to link Toronto with Chicago—despite strenuous opposition from the Cornelius Vanderbilt interests, who controlled the Michigan Central Railroad.

This group was late off the mark to the Soo, however, and did not have the ear of the current Canadian government. Their financing was also in doubt.

The formidable and deep-pocketed Vanderbilt, now a sworn enemy of the Grand Trunk, was the fourth force. His Michigan Central had announced plans to construct a big new railroad ferry from St. Ignace across the Mackinac Strait, which would allow McMillan's DSS&A to transfer 38 freight cars of Duluth flour at a time via the Michigan Central south through Detroit and eastward from there. Vanderbilt's group would be delighted if the bridge never happened, and it had an eye on purchasing the entire DSS&A.

On February 12, 1887, William Washburn, who had been the congressman from Minneapolis from 1879 through 1885 (see Chapter 6 for Washburn's political career), returned to Minneapolis from lengthy negotiations in Washington, D.C. He announced to the press that the new bridge would be a joint venture of four companies: the Soo Line and the DSS&A in the United States and the Canadian Pacific and Grand Trunk in Canada. In the background, the Vanderbilt group began preparing a bid to buy the DSS&A.

Back in the Wisconsin woods, in February's snowdrifts northwest of Rhinelander, Captain Rich and engineer Willis at last selected a route and location for the bridge over the Wisconsin River. For the second winter in a row, construction crews raced to get piles driven before the ice went out. A few weeks later, the Henry and Balch construction firm moved crews and equipment to Saunders Point on Lake Michigan. William Washburn, who liked naming things, tagged the place "Gladstone," after the British prime minister. (He probably thought that the name would be a nice touch, not only because of the British and Canadian money now backing the line, but because of the quantity of flour that would be moving through destined for housewives across Britain.) Rich's construction headquarters moved east to Rhinelander, and again a tiny place deep in the woods blossomed with new sidings, new buildings, and mountains of ties, telegraph poles, pilings, and bridge timber.

For the Michigan leg of the job, there were hundreds of streams and swamps to cross. (In a pond along the route outside Hermansville called Malacca, quicksand still has been known to swallow wandering cattle.) As much as 20 percent of this section would have to be bridged. A sawmill in Ludington, Michigan, was contracted there to furnish three million feet of bridge timber. Between Rhinelander and Gladstone alone, over 11,000 feet of culvert plus 81 bridges were built. This means that about 5 percent of this 126-mile section had to be built in the air.

The new port of Gladstone appeared as if by magic during 1887. Construction included a large station, another roundhouse, a machine shop, merchandise and coal docks, and an iron ore dock 768 feet long, plus a rail approach of another 914 feet. None of this included the town, which, like most of the depots on the whole route, attracted settlers almost instantly. Business for the facility and badly-needed westbound freight for the railroad was insured in February through an alliance with the Lehigh Valley Company to use its fleet of seven colliers to bring in Pennsylvania coal for the Twin Cities market.

The final miles into Sault Ste. Marie were a relative breeze. The land was flat, requiring far less grading and bridgework than the sections already crossed. With thousands of men at work and each section already cleared of trees, a routine was established that ate up the miles. The road was completed to Trout Lake in November, but winter was right behind them.

The settlement of Sault Ste. Marie had spent every winter of the last two hundred years in isolation—from November 15, when the last southbound vessel cleared the canal and the lakes froze up, to around April 1, when ice breakup usually allowed the first vessel northbound. Now the town not only got a railroad. In one short period, it got three of them.[37] Now travelers could get from this outpost east to Montreal or west to Duluth or Minneapolis all year long in a matter of hours instead of weeks.

On a snowy January morning in 1888, the huddled welcoming committee at the Sault Ste. Marie depot would greet not one but two trains bearing the men who made this miracle happen. From the west out

---

37   The Soo Line, the Canadian Pacific, and, in September, the Duluth, South Shore and Atlantic.

of the gloom, and plastered in snow from its cowcatcher to its diamond-shaped smokestack, came a hooting, hissing wood-burning engine. It pulled a train of just two cars. Its engineer, squinting out the open window of his cab, looked as frost-rhymed as the Ancient Mariner himself. And indeed he had good reason to be. He had brought his special cargo the long way from Minneapolis—more than five hundred miles through forest wilderness in the dead of winter. His was the first train to complete the entire route from one end to the other. In the two coaches, the windows were sealed with thick frost from the cold outside and red-hot stoves inside. Fittingly, this special train was carrying most of the special group of men who had made the dream happen, through every conceivable high and low, since William's brother Israel had first described the vision almost 15 years before.

First off the train was a conductor, bundled up in overcoat and muffler, bearing a shovel with which he did his best to clear the snow and ice off the coach steps down to the station platform. Shouldering past him in their eagerness were the two men most responsible for the tiny train being there: William Washburn and Capt. Watson Rich.

They almost had not made it. A Milwaukee newspaper reported on December 21 that a train full of Soo Line directors and executives, travelling "at a very high rate of speed," had smashed into a Wisconsin Central southbound freight train at Prentice, where the two lines crossed, completely destroying two freight cars.[38] Then three feet of snow had fallen across northern Michigan. It had taken another train pushing a huge plow, plus a second engine pushing a flanger, to clear between the rails and set back the tops of the huge piles left by the first engine, plus a crew of 20 men to clear the track for the bigwigs soon to be charging through the woods behind them.

Rocking along between 25 and 40 miles an hour, Washburn and Rich had made the trip in just over a day. It had taken millions of dollars,

---

38 *Milwaukee Sentinel*, December 22, 1887. High speed was typical for the railroad moguls of the day. *The Sault Ste. Marie News* of June 1, 1889, reported that Van Horne's special Canadian Pacific train had made it from the Sault to Gladstone in just under four hours, for an average of about 58 miles per hour, and then all the way to St. Paul in just over 13 hours. Considering the primitive conditions of track and ballast at the time, this must have been a hair-raising ride.

Minnesota Historical Society

Keeping a railroad functioning in the Upper Midwest offered challenges like this one that a Chicago and Northwestern crew dealt with in 1880—after they got the track cleared.

thousands of men, and four hard years of work, but Washburn's vision was at last a reality. The millers of Minneapolis had their own route to the Soo. However cold that day in Sault Ste. Marie, it was William's day in the sun.

That same day, from the other direction, Canada, across the long bridge that had only been completed five days earlier, came a second train with two cars: a business car followed by the "Matapedia," which the local newspaper labeled a "palace car."[39] From it stepped a galaxy of Canada's most prominent railroad men: Canadian Pacific general manager William Cornelius Van Horne, his assistant Thomas D. Shaughnessy, solicitor R. M.

---

39 *Sault Ste. Marie News*, January 7, 1888. Van Horne was famous for his luxurious "palace cars," in which he travelled at top speed over his railroad empire. Large plate-glass windows, ornately carved mahogany woodwork, plush upholstery, a private kitchen, and delicate etched glass provided spectacular surroundings for the most important people in Canada—plus the boss's poker games and violin recitals. The *Matapedia* had a particularly hard life, and after being burned, rebuilt, and renamed, it was destroyed by a rock slide in British Columbia in 1925. *Canadian Rail*, July-August, 1983.

Bayliss Library, Sault Ste. Marie, Michigan

The dream realized: With this international bridge completed, Canadian engines could push strings of freight cars loaded with Minneapolis flour across the St. Mary's River on their way to eastern and international markets.

Welles, directors Sir Donald Smith and Richard J. Cross, chief engineer W. A. Ramsey, and assistant superintendent B. W. Coyne. These were the men who, as they had promised, had brought the CP hundreds of miles to the Canadian side of the border and helped make possible the long bridge across the St. Mary's River. The last hundred miles of the route had been a tough nut to crack because the north shore of Lake Huron had proven to be almost solid pre-Cambrian rock, and they had had to blast through all of it at a cost of $20,000 per mile. But the cigar-chomping, poker-playing Van Horne would be stopped by no obstacle, and the route was completed as it had been promised.

In the background, the Grand Trunk Railroad had been left in the dust. Its charter to build to the Sault had expired, and it never exercised its right to buy one quarter of the CP's share of the bridge.

And what an impressive work the bridge was. Over a mile long, it consisted of 10 enormous spans on 11 huge stone piers, plus a swing bridge over the shipping canal. Each span stretched 242 feet and weighed

260 tons. The first stone had been set in place on the Canadian side just seven months before. The ironwork, started in October, had been completed December 31. After the early winter twilight had turned dark, the first trains crossed the new span.

A reporter at the event noted that Van Horne, "round and rosy," and Washburn, "angular and stern." After crossing over to the tiny settlement on the Canadian side, they went for a sleigh ride together.

While it was much too cold and uncomfortable to sponsor his preferred celebratory trainload of brass bands and newspaper reporters, Washburn wasted no time in demonstrating what the whole project had been about. Logs, lumber, and iron ore might help pay some of the new line's bills, but the real pay-off was to be flour. Before he had even climbed aboard the special train, he had made plans for a spectacular debut of the Minneapolis, Sault Ste. Marie and Atlantic Railroad, soon to be known simply as the Soo Line.

On the same day that Washburn hobnobbed with the Canadians at Sault Ste. Marie, a mammoth flour train left Minneapolis's mills with 102 freight cars crammed to the roof with flour. The train was in five sections, from five different mills, to symbolize the millers' long dream. Despite it being winter, Lake Superior being closed at Duluth, and rail traffic being snarled in hostile Chicago, this train would carry 20 carloads from Charles A. Pillsbury's mill to Boston, 20 more from William's Washburn Mill Company to New York, 20 more from Washburn-Crosby to New York, another 20 from Sidle, Fletcher and Holmes to Philadelphia, and a final 20 from Pettit, Christian and Co. ultimately to London and Glasgow, Scotland.

The first of the five sections arrived in Sault Ste. Marie in the afternoon on Sunday, January 8, and the last section arrived early the next morning. Within a few hours, each section was taken in tow by a CP engine and crew. The first one arrived in Boston, via Montreal, on the morning of January 12—just one week after leaving the Pillsbury mill. The trip had been faster and had cost less than ever paid before.

Despite cold weather in the East a crowd of two thousand hardy souls was at the Sault to see the first section come in. People read out the jubilant signs attached to almost every boxcar: "Minnesota Sends Greetings to New England," "Go west, young man, and grow up with the country," "New England is the place to be born in, but Minnesota is the place to live in," and "First Through-Shipment to the Seaboard." The exuberant words underlined the differences between the millers' and other rail operators' attitudes toward competition. Whereas other railroads were locked in a do-or-die struggle for dominance, the millers were acting together, without government involvement, for their joint benefit. One of their first moves upon completion of the road was to announce a reduction in rates for shipping flour.

Because Canadian and British money had made the millers' dream come true, many people—especially outmaneuvered railroad interests in Chicago—questioned the fact that foreigners were gaining control of railroads critical to the Midwest. This concern reached the halls of Congress in 1888, but because people in Minneapolis were so happy with the new service, jingoistic rhetoric quickly died. Chicagoans had to accept being bypassed. Milwaukee's flour-milling industry slowly declined. William's brother Cadwallader, now five years in his grave, would have smiled.

Before long the U.S. government inadvertently provided the Soo line with a further advantage. In April 1887, Congress introduced controls over some freight rates through its new Interstate Commerce Commission. The law had been brought on by increasing protests against rate inequities practiced by railroad operators in Chicago acting in concert. It made "pooling" and rebates illegal and required all rates be reasonable and equitable. Since there was no such regulation of rates in Canada, railroads there could set rates as low as they wanted—lower than American rates. Since nearly half of the Soo Line route east ran through Canada, the Soo could charge their customers less because its route was shorter and Canadian rates were lower. By 1890, as the millers' total production topped a whopping seven million barrels, they had insured themselves of the least expensive, shortest, and fastest route to the East Coast.

Business on the new line boomed. The owners beamed. In Canada, with the huge CP project finally complete to the Pacific, Van Horne quietly consolidated his gains and moved to relieve his banker friends of any qualms they might have over their Soo Line loans. Details were not made public, but on June 11, 1888, the four companies that William had created to get the rails from the Soo to the Dakotas were consolidated under the single name "Minneapolis, St. Paul and Sault Ste. Marie Railroad," and the CP took over the new company's debts, together with 51 percent of its stock.

Later that summer, the Canadians had another victory. The McMillan group announced on July 14 that they had sold their entire DSS&A system to the CP, despite furious opposition from the Michigan Central and its Vanderbilt backers. After the DSS&A link from Duluth to Sault Ste. Marie was completed in September, year-round flour traffic from both Minneapolis and Duluth would rumble over the new bridge under the benevolent control of the Canadians.

Both McMillan and Washburn would move on to other things—including seats in the U.S. Senate. Vanderbilt and the Grand Trunk were shut out of the Upper Midwest, and the Canadians had run the table on railroading in Upper Michigan.

Prudently, Van Horne kept a very low profile. American management of the Soo Line, including the colorful Frederick D. Underwood, was retained, and Captain Rich was given the means to improve the merged lines. By 1889, the Soo Line owned 62 locomotives—coal burners costing more than $6,000 each—together with 2,636 box cars and 35 cabooses with the Soo logo on them. It would be another 50 years, during the Great Depression of the 1930s, before the Canadians actually took over operation of Soo Line and 80 years after that before logos painted on the line's rolling stock began to change. In the meantime, the Bank of Montreal would realize an excellent source of income, the millers of Minneapolis would have an independent outlet for their product, and Canadians would have a shipping alternative if anything ever went wrong with the long CP route just completed north of Lake Superior.

The road also helped fulfill the vision of William Washburn's brother Israel for the future of the port of Portland, Maine. As the *Northwestern Miller* reported in 1899, the number of ocean steamers visiting that port annually had increased from 57 to 120 in the previous five years, total exports were over 15,000 freight car loads annually, and the Grand Trunk railroad from Montreal could now store over 1.1 million bushels of grain in its new dockside elevators there.[40]

---

40 *Northwestern Miller*, March 6, 1899, p. 439.

With the CP now controlling the Soo, William was replaced as president,[41] although he retained his place on the board for the rest of his life. Once again, he had made a big dream come true, and someone else would make it work.

The millers were probably relieved. Although they would realize rich benefits from the new road, they would never have to learn how to run it. The new owners poured support into the line, and its performance attracted new investors. By the end of 1899, Soo Line stocks and bonds totaled $41 million in value.

Considering time, territory, and obstacles along the way, the completion of the Minneapolis, Sault Ste. Marie and Atlantic Railroad—the Soo Line—was one of the greatest railroad construction feats in the United States. Between 1883 and 1888, 722 miles of railroad, not counting sidings and switching yards, had been built through the wilderness.

William Washburn was probably glad to dance away from the details of the enormous enterprise he had created. His heavy-lifting partner Captain Rich would stay on to help the new owners strengthen the line to carry the traffic it attracted, including more than a million barrels of flour in the first year alone. But the dancer had several even bigger things ahead. He was 57 years old and still full of energy. He would have several more great moments, including several in the political arena—a world he had courted since he first arrived in Minneapolis.

---

41 *Sault Ste. Marie News*, September 21, 1889, used the verb "deposed."

6

The Rockets' Not So Red Glare
1860–1895

The chairman was outraged. "That means the death of the Republican Party," he bellowed.[42] *Senator George F. Hoar, with his colleague Henry Cabot Lodge, both scions of proper Boston and bearers of the Republican torch carried since the Civil War, had just seen their final hope of a Federal Elections bill— and two years of hard work—go down to defeat in the U.S. Senate for the second and final time. The 1891 motion—which would prove to be the last effort to secure African American voting rights in the South for the next 75 years—went down to defeat by a vote of 35 to 34. By the luck of the alphabet, the last and tie-breaking vote that killed the bill was made by Minnesota's Senator William Washburn.*

American politics is sometimes hereditary. In families like the Adamses, the Roosevelts, and the Kennedys, public service calls one generation after another. In the case of Maine's Washburn family, the inheritance in a single generation was extraordinary. William Washburn had been surrounded by politics almost since birth. His father Israel and his uncle Reuel had served the town of Livermore, Maine, for more than 50 years. As justice of the peace, his father had settled most of the quarrels in the neighborhood over his dining room table. His sons moved on to larger stages.

William, age 19 when his oldest brother, Israel, was first elected to Congress, witnessed from close-range three brothers helping to get the Republican Party off the ground, there and at home. Thereafter, from his summer jobs in Washington, D.C., to his earliest days in Minneapolis, William had never been far from the halls of power.

---

42   Fred Wellborn, "The Influence of the Silver Republican Senators," *Mississippi Valley Historical Review*, 14 (March 1928): 479.

Washburn's vote that day in 1891— though directly opposed to the will of party leaders including President Benjamin Harrison—did not really "kill" the Republican Party. In no way was William a political maverick at heart. But his vote did mark a significant milepost in the party's long journey away from the high moral ground on which it had fought the Civil War, ended slavery, and pursued Reconstruction in the South. The country had had enough social engineering.

The defeat of the "Force Bill," as Democrats called it, also marked a strong reaffirmation of both parties' commitment to the country's commercial interests. This included a tariff that encouraged trade as well as protected local industries, "free silver" to benefit the mining interests in the new states of the West, and a reaffirmation of the political status quo for the sake of economic recovery in the South. No matter how desirable voting rights might be from a moral point of view, by the early 1890s Americans no longer had the fire to change the society of any region of the country. A boom of internationalism was about to begin, and New England's long moral crusade was being submerged in a nation that wanted its government to encourage the unfettered pursuit of profit or to get out of its way. Despite the moral trajectory of his upbringing, William Washburn perfectly represented this sentiment.

Washburn's three congressman brothers would probably have been appalled by Young Rapid's vote. But they were gone now—Israel in his grave for nearly 20 years. It was a new era with new priorities. The Republican Party still dominated the country, but it no longer elected evangelists. Its standard-bearers came from the new elite, and they expected to be in office what they had been out of office—honest, God-fearing, respectable, competent, successful, and noncontroversial. Washburn was, by 1889, all of these things.

From the spirited discussions around the dinner table, the much-read copies of three newspapers subscribed to by the family, and the frequent letters received from his absent older brothers, William had been a fascinated (and opinionated) student of public affairs. He took eagerly to the summer experiences in Washington arranged for him by his brothers. He graduated in the same month that the awful Kansas-Nebraska Bill passed—an event that caused his family, including its three sitting congressmen, to give up on their beloved Whig Party. In his law studies in Bangor, he saw Israel bring the new Republican Party to dominance in Maine in 1856. William had been in Minnesota less than a year when the territory became a state. Although only 27, William had even won a seat in the legislature, until it was redistricted out of existence by the new state constitution.

Perhaps as compensation, he was picked to be a part of the Minnesota Republican delegation that went to Chicago and nominated the little-known Abraham Lincoln for the presidency in 1860. Israel Jr. had originally favored William E. Seward, an old friend and colleague. Young William and his brother Elihu, who had known Lincoln

Minnesota Historical Society
William's Washburn's populist political opponent, Ignatius Donnelly, 1870.

since 1842, might have had something to do with bringing their older brother over to Lincoln. As a "Wide Awake" marcher in Minneapolis, William was certainly a part of the anti-slaveholder excitement and fervor that marked that 1860 election campaign.

The Washburn brothers' support for Lincoln may have helped secure William the post of state surveyor general in 1861, a job that kept William out of the army and gave him the title "General." Operating from the St. Paul capital, General Washburn spent most of the next three years surveying agricultural land and timber lots and platting new towns for future immigrants—as well as adding acreage to his own portfolio. Between this work and keeping construction going at St. Anthony Falls and promoting the industrial sites being created there, William developed contacts among movers and shakers all over the state. In 1864, he again threw his hat into the ring for election to the state legislature. He lost—to a colorful gad-fly named Ignatius Donnelly.

Washburn and Donnelly were fated to bedevil each other for the next 30 years. They could not have been more opposite. The choice of the

Republican political establishment in Minneapolis, Washburn had strengths that included an immaculate appearance, an aura of noblesse oblige, careful logic, honesty, and a handsome wife. Donnelly, an opportunistic Irishman, was short, quick witted, outrageous in debate, and a natural showman who loved a fight. There was no establishment he did not enjoy attacking or an office he would not run for. Fearless, he would change parties as necessary and put on a show wherever he went. He had no scruples about personally profiting from any office he might win. He loved to campaign. Party regulars came to hate him.

Donnelly became Minnesota's elected lieutenant governor in 1860. He resigned the position when he was elected to Congress as a Republican in 1862. Washburn served the first of three terms on the Minneapolis School Committee beginning in 1866, when Donnelly was re-elected to Congress for a third term. There, on the floor of the House of Representatives in 1868, Donnelly had a spectacular run-in with William's older brother Elihu. One afternoon, to the delight of the members present, the two traded so many personal insults that the *New York Times* castigated both of them. One consequence of the brouhaha was that, in the concurrent Senate impeachment trial of President Andrew Johnson, the charge that the president used intemperate language and brought disrespect to Congress was quietly dropped. Leaders apparently decided that people in glass houses shouldn't throw stones.

Singed by the fall-out from this affair, Minnesota Republicans nominated William to run for Donnelly's congressional seat that year. A defiant Donnelly bolted the party, taking his supporters with him, and determined to run as an independent Republican. The idea of a split in his party was entirely too messy for William. He declined the nomination to run against the maverick, and Democrats went on to win the seat. The following year Donnelly—overlooking the fact that his bolt had caused the party's defeat—unsuccessfully tried to win the Republican nomination for governor. The party had had enough of the gadfly.

William's political fortunes, on the other hand, improved. He was elected to his long sought-after state legislature seat in 1871. There he was active in securing legislation to give the state some measure of control over the railroads—including freight rates. In 1873 his old friend George

Brackett was elected mayor of Minneapolis. William missed out being nominated for the governor's chair by a single vote. Afterwards, a miscount was discovered that would have given him the nomination, but he declined to pursue the issue for fear of causing dissention in the party. This move strengthened his standing with Republican leaders and paved the way for his second nomination in 1876 to run again for Congress from Minnesota's Third District. This time William accepted the nomination. His opponent in the election was again Donnelly, who had discovered populism as his new road to office and the Democratic Party as his own.

Theirs was a classic confrontation: a populist country demagogue versus an establishment city businessman. The contested district was enormous, stretching from well below Minneapolis to north of Duluth. This 1876 congressional contest became known as the "Brass Kettle" campaign, after the instrument commonly used to weigh grain at the railroad elevators. Washburn coolly countered all of Donnelly's accusations that his railroad—the Minneapolis and St. Louis—was cheating farmers. The system for weighing grain was fair. His freight rates had always been lower than any other line.

Their debate was a contest of proven fact against emotional rhetoric. Washburn won the election over the "calamity howlers" handily.[43] He also won Donnelly's court challenge afterwards, when Donnelly's lawyer was found to have forged key evidence in the case. William went on to be re-elected to Congress two more times. He was the fourth Washburn brother to be elected and re-elected to Congress and from a fourth different state.

This campaign, and both Cadwallader's and William's steady record of support for farmers' interests, reflected something about the millers' philosophy of doing business. Their business was the farmers' business. Their mills could not exist without farmers' wheat and without a fair means of getting wheat from farm to mill. Both Cadwallader and William solidly favored government control over railroad rates—heretical views among competing railroad operators. The Washburns' business was essentially flour milling, and their interest in railroading was purely an adjunct. This made them unique among railroaders and difficult targets

---

43 *Minneapolis Journal*, Silver Anniversary edition, November 26, 1903.

for populists who would become a force among Minnesota and Wisconsin farmers.

William was not the glad-handing prototype of a gilded-age politician, however. His youngest son Stanley remembered his father "was not a politician and refused to compromise or trade with anyone in the state. . . . In those days character and moral courage brought the votes; he evidently had both."[44]

Formal as he may have been, William's record in the six years he served in Congress reflected the wishes of a business-oriented constituency—both city and farm—that had elected him. But it was a record that jars modern-day sensibilities. In 1882 he spoke in favor of limiting Chinese immigration to the country to protect free labor from being "degraded" by 20-cents-an-hour competition. Two years later he joined with new Congressman Knute Nelson in support of a bill to move 1,200 Ojibwe (Chippewa) Indians off their Red Lake Reservation in order to open up three million acres of forest and agricultural lands to development. Although his goal in Congress was efficient use of resources, he spoke and wrote with the casual arrogance and racism of his age. The Chinese, a "semi-barbarous civilization," had "never assimilated with the Anglo-Saxon race" and were "unaffected by the Christian religion and the high civilization that has followed it everywhere." Chinese workers were "the lowest and most disgusting class of cheap labor that has ever cursed this country." Native Minnesota Ojibwe were "miserable, wretched vagabonds," and he agreed with Nelson that they should be moved where they could be brought under "civilizing and Christianizing influence."[45]

William's words were accepted by his constituents without comment in the 1880s—despite the fact that 20 years earlier many had risked lives and fortunes fighting to preserve the Union where all men were created equal. Clearly, after Reconstruction fizzled in the fog that followed the hung presidential election of 1876, the reformist fire had gone out of the Republican Party. Social engineering was bad for business.

---

44 Stanley Washburn, Sr., unpublished autobiography, 1947, Washburn Family Papers.
45 Congressional Record, 8: 2161–63 and 15: 2740.

Then William found the perfect issue to benefit most of his constituents—including himself. Despite many improvements to his dam and waterpower canal at the Falls of St. Anthony, mill and factory owners on both sides of the Mississippi still suffered from seasonal fluctuations in the river's water level. During dry summers, low levels of water meant less water available to power machinery. That meant less production for the tenants and fewer fees for the landlord.

While growing up in Maine, William had learned a bit about dams and water storage. As surveyor general, he had become familiar with the large northern lakes that fed the Mississippi. He realized that a series of strategically located upstream dams at the lakes' outlets could control the flow and level of the entire Mississippi River. Once spring's high water levels were locked behind dams, water could be released as needed during dry summer and fall months. Not only would these controlled levels be good for the businesses that depended on the river, but they would control floods far downstream. Augmented by strategically located piers and dikes along the river banks, these dams could also produce more reliable channels for river shipping—including the long-held dream of extending the head of navigation upriver from St. Paul to Minneapolis. As early as 1869, William had in fact purchased land at a dam site along a gorge below the outlet of Lake Pokegama in northern Itasca County with an eye toward future use.

An entire system of Mississippi watershed dams would cost far more than the millers could pay, but it would be a viable project for the federal government. So William initiated the necessary legislation, securing an appropriation in 1880 that provided $150,000 to get started. Over the next 15 years, he paved the way for $2 million in federal funding for a series of upstream dams and navigational aids on the Mississippi—to the benefit of every mill and steamboat line in Minnesota and in Wisconsin and Iowa as well. As it turned out, these reservoirs would be his most lasting public monuments.

The widely visible work was well under way when William decided not to run for a fourth term in Congress. This may have had something to do with the stand he took against the Morrison Tariff bill that proposed reducing national import tariffs by 20 percent. While his vote followed his party's old national platform supporting protection of U.S. goods, it ran counter to the stand by Minnesota's four other Republican congressmen, as well as his own business interests. (His railroad was paying 50 percent more to buy the finest German steel rails because of the steep tariff on imports.) Imposing high tariffs on imports was no way to encourage his new legions of overseas flour buyers, either. They would expect the same access to American markets that he was getting in theirs.

For whatever reasons William decided to come home in 1882—perhaps to repair political fences but definitely to submerge himself in many business affairs. His departure from Congress was noted this way in the *Northwestern Miller*: "By the time this issue reaches the majority of our readers, the congressional career of Hon. W. D. Washburn will have closed. . . . He is head and shoulders above any man ever sent from the North Star state, and none appreciate this fact better than his brother millers."[46]

William was far from finished with politics, however. Although he held no elected office between 1882 and 1888, he kept his eye on that choicest of political goals —a seat in the U.S. Senate. The challenge for him, as it was for his brothers, was that U.S. senators were not elected directly by a state's citizens, but by state legislatures.

In nearly every state legislature, elections for senator were the most exciting battles that happened. The glad handing, the horse trading, the back stabbing, the settling of old scores, the patronage promises were spectacular. During these uproars, even the remotest backcountry legislator felt briefly like a kingmaker. Aspirants had to lay the groundwork for their candidacies years in advance.

In the late nineteenth century, senatorial elections were particularly vulnerable to machine politics. Perceived unreliability to carry out the wishes of a particular political boss brought quick and repeated death to the hopes of many a good man—including those of William's brothers Israel (before James G. Blaine's machine in Maine) and Elihu (against the machinations of "Black Jack" Logan in Illinois). Even blunt-talking Cadwallader had been unsuccessful in at least two different tries for a senate seat in Wisconsin because of opposition from his railroad rival, Alexander Mitchell of the Milwaukee Road.

---

46 *Northwestern Miller*, February 27, 1885, p. 198.

William, between the end of his last term in Congress and the time of the next available Senate seat, had plenty of time to grease the skids of the Minnesota state legislature. The incumbent senator was lumberman Dwight Sabin of Stillwater, whose own somewhat tainted victory over incumbent William Windom six years earlier still rankled the memories of many a Republican regular. Meanwhile, William's many works were already beginning to show benefits to the public. His federally-provided upstream reservoirs were improving waterpower at the falls, and his Soo Line railroad had just opened to make another long-held Minnesota dream come true. William's lieutenants, including the faithful W. D. Hale, scouted for supporters. Thanks to William's experience and record of good works, there were many supporters to be found—including an up-and-coming Alexandria politician named Knute Nelson. Washburn had helped the young Norwegian farmer-lawyer get support among key Republicans in Minneapolis to win his Fifth District seat in Congress in 1882, and he would help him again when Nelson won the governorship in 1892.

Incumbent Sabin's support had weakened during his six years in Washington, despite support from his friend and ally, James J. Hill. As the day for the vote approached at St. Paul, Hill was even called to Washington to confer with President Cleveland and other Democratic leaders about how, with the irrepressible Ignatius Donnelly as their candidate, they could stop Washburn's election. But it was too late. When the roll was called in January 1889, William was the clear winner. Donnelly reportedly "stomped out of the chamber, snorting that it was the worst legislature ever known."[47] William, the darling of both conservative businessmen and progressive-minded farmers, was the first Washburn brother to be elected to the U.S. Senate. Not long afterwards, Major Hale was appointed postmaster for Minneapolis, with the power to fill more government jobs than any other position in the state.

William was not the darling of everyone out on the prairies. A month after his victory, a fire-eating editor in North Dakota estimated that Washburn's election cost him $250,000 in payments of many legislators' campaign expenses. The new senator, he wrote, "is at the head of the wheat ring, at the head of the pineland and lumber ring, holds railroad

---

47   Martin, *J. J. Hill*, 306.

stocks watered to the amount of $17,000,000 and the late acquisition places him at the head of the Republican machine in Minnesota. . . . No one seriously denies that boodle carried the day."[48]

William's tolerance for political infighting was limited. The pushing and pulling in the legislature necessary to win the election was far rougher than he had known. The deals made and unmade, the back-door negotiating, and the general kowtowing to the most remote representatives left him exhausted. After his tumultuous victory, he staggered home to Fair Oaks, his Minneapolis home. A newspaper noted "the greatest apprehension of his family and friends concerning his recovery. . . . his nervous system was unable to sustain the tension to which it was subjected."[49] Happily, recuperation was swift, and he and Lizzie packed their bags and led the family entourage back to Washington. After nearly 30 years of trying, in the legislatures of four different states, on March 4, 1889, a Washburn finally took his seat in the U.S. Senate.

While William and Lizzie rubbed elbows with the mighty in the nation's capital, a populist revolution was brewing back in Minnesota. Outside the Republican power elites in city and county seat organizations, political antagonism and protests had been building in townships and on farms. Protest came in the form of the Farmers Alliance, which by 1890 had blossomed into more than 1,200 sub-alliances across the state. In 1892, Knute Nelson, skillfully positioning himself as the Republicans' best hope against the alliance, won election to the governorship. His opponent: Ignatius Donnelly, this time representing the Progressive Party. Again, Senator Washburn introduced and supported Nelson in Minneapolis. What both William and his supporters were slow to realize was that, when Nelson was elected, a wave of followers swept with him into the legislature—all of whom were independent of traditional Republican party leaders, current government job holders, and farmers.

In the Senate, William's first effort reflected a progressive cause. He waged war on commodity speculators whose increasing manipulations on the grain exchange in Chicago were affecting the price of foods to the

---

48   *Wahpeton Times,* February 7, 1889.

49   *Delano Eagle,* January 31, 1889.

detriment of producers. An "Options" bill to do away with the system sailed through the House, passed the Senate with some minor alteration, then was buried and killed back in the House by its formidable speaker, Thomas B. Reed. (A manuscript fragment in William's handwriting includes his observation: "Mr. Reed is ugly and perverse. I cannot account for his conduct on any ground except that of original sin."[50])

The year 1890 brought the climax to the long campaign over a Federal Elections bill, called the "Force" bill by its Democratic opponents, that would allow blacks to vote in federal elections. "Integrity and purity of elections" had been part of the Republican national platform in 1888, and President Harrison had given his blessing to the initiative. A Republican caucus had approved a Federal Elections bill which passed the house and reached the Senate in December 1890—at about the same time as a free-silver bill much favored by several new senators from recently admitted western states. These so-called "silver Republicans," together with Washburn, joined with Democrat opposition to put aside the "Force" bill. By a narrow vote, the senators voted to take up the bill again after a silver bill had been passed, but the elections bill failed for a second time by a single vote. That vote was William Washburn's.

Oddly, there was virtually no public outcry at this outcome. It was simply noted with interest that Democrats had found maverick Republicans to help them defeat an important Republican issue. The dominant concern of the time remained tariffs, and Republicans were still firmly in control on that front. It would be 65 years before the Senate again considered letting blacks vote.

William was unapologetic about his vote. He defended it for being in the best interests of trade and for avoiding government-enforced hardship on the South. He even wrote one constituent that his party was not in touch with the people of the country on this issue and that "the better class of Republicans in Minnesota" did not want Southern whites forced to open their elections to blacks,[51] sentiments apparently received with equanimity. The Republicans had been in power long enough to develop

---

50   Unsigned letter, June 7, 1898, Washburn Family Papers.

51   Theodore A. Webb, *"Washburn, A Pivotal Figure,"* unpublished essay provided to author.

a hierarchy of respectability, and William's comment underscored an assumed mutual understanding with his correspondent. As he had no doubt learned from providing summertime lodging to southern visitors at his hotel on Lake Minnetonka, the "better class" of southerners deserved the same treatment as the "better class" of northerners. How far this was from his family's passions of just 35 years earlier!

Much later, William's son Stanley provided a further explanation for his father's vote. He wrote that the Force bill was "a reversion to the days of reconstruction" and that, just as Elihu had fought against radicals after the Civil War and had "favored every measure to help the South recuperate," so his father wished to do nothing to interrupt this same recuperation 22 years later. (Stanley was apparently unaware that Elihu, during the impeachment trial of President Johnson, had turned radical himself.)[52]

William's Senate career contained another highlight in 1891. After a terrible wheat crop in Russia, William C. Edgar, the brilliant and persuasive editor of the *Northwestern Miller*, urged flour millers across the country to donate millions of pounds of flour to stave off starvation by 30 million Russian peasants. In Minneapolis, the Pillsbury-Washburn mills led the way with a gift of more than 100,000 pounds of flour to the Millers Russian Relief Movement. In Washington, William shepherded a bill through the Senate that authorized the U.S. Navy to carry the precious cargo, but isolationism and mistrust of Russia's inefficient government led to its defeat in the House. Then a shipping line volunteered one of its vessels, and on April 3, 1892, the first shipload was successfully delivered and distributed. It was eventually followed by four others. In all, more than five million pounds of American flour were distributed throughout Russia. Czar Alexander III personally thanked William for his help in the matter.[53]

Back in Minnesota in June 1892, Republicans brought their national convention to Minneapolis. It would be held in the large new building that William had helped create for the Great Industrial Exposition of 1888. Senator Washburn, his old friend George Brackett, and his former

---

52 Stanley Washburn, Sr., unpublished autobiography, 25.

53 Edgar's campaign is described in Harold F. Smith, "Bread for the Russians," in *Minnesota History*, Summer, 1970.

Minnesota Historical Society

Senator William Washburn helped persuade Republicans to bring the national convention to the new Exposition Building in Minneapolis in 1892, the first political convention held west of Chicago. Republicans did not return to the Twin Cities until 2008.

partner Thomas Lowry were influential in the decision. "We need this convention," William told party leaders, "to stimulate the fresh energies of the Republican Party."[54] They got the convention—the first time either national party had met west of Chicago. George Brackett was tasked with organizing and managing the event. Alas, despite Brackett's best juggling of limited hotel space and inadequate rail transportation, the convention ended early, and local eating and sleeping establishments got less business than they had hoped for.

William and his palatial Fair Oaks residence were at the heart of the convention. With enormous American flags fluttering from five different flag poles around the place, he and Lizzie entertained party bigwigs and proudly showed off their castle. Nominee Benjamin Harrison was one of

---

54   June Denning Holmquist, "Convention City, The Republicans in Minneapolis, 1892," in *Minnesota History*, June 1956, p. 68.

three presidents and past-presidents entertained at the mansion during the event.

Despite the fact that Harrison was the incumbent president, however, neither he nor his main competitor, James G. Blaine, were able to stimulate much delegate enthusiasm. In November. Democrat Grover Cleveland defeated Harrison by almost half a million votes.

This was also the year that Knute Nelson won the governorship of the state with William's support. Progressives were challenging the Republican establishment in Minnesota, and Nelson was seen as the best hope of defeating them. Two years later, with labor unrest in the cities adding to the progressive din in the countryside and the establishment fearing radicalism and anarchy, Nelson was re-elected governor. The Washburn forces, perhaps now more attentive to their man's stature on the national scene, were less attentive than they should have been as Nelson strengthened his support in the state legislature and doled out still more jobs to his supporters.

Republican political waters in Minnesota were also muddied by scandal related to timber valuations never performed. The reputations of a number of prominent Republicans including both John Pillsbury and Senator Washburn were threatened. In addition, following a terrible forest fire that obliterated the town of Hinckley in 1894, people charged government laxity in regulating practices of the lumber industry.

Despite these problems, as William's term in the Senate neared its end, he remained the clear favorite for reelection. Six reservoir dams on the Mississippi had been completed, and his followers across the city and county organizations were mobilized. But he also had powerful enemies who were eager to finance a campaign to defeat him. The Chicago Board of Trade was wary that he might try to revive his effort against commodity speculators. James J. Hill was angry at him for building the Soo Line so close to Hill's Manitoba lines to the Dakotas. The *New York Times* observed that Governor Nelson had 47 votes already pledged to him. Nelson's lieutenant governor, D. M. Clough, was also eager to work for Nelson so he could succeed to the governor's chair.

On January 3, 1895, Washburn's old political ally, Governor Nelson, announced his bid for William's seat. Washburn and his main-line

Republican supporters were thunderstruck. They claimed treachery—that Nelson had given his word not to run. William rushed to the governor's office to confront him, where he got the news face-to-face. Nelson was in the race, and Nelson intended to win. Newspapers roundly castigated him, but the Norwegian just grew more determined. There followed the famous Three Week War in the Minnesota legislature. It was a classic confrontation: establishment versus anti-establishment, city versus country, native versus immigrant, insider versus outsider, aristocrat versus man of the people—with every shade of promise and threat that money, influence, rhetoric, and effort could provide. The first vote in the legislature took place on January 18. Of 72 votes needed, Washburn got a disappointing 61, Nelson 45. In subsequent days, Nelson gradually eroded Washburn's lead. Finally, in a joint session of both houses on January 23, Nelson won the decisive vote. The anti-Washburn forces, which included a powerful combination of populist Scandinavian farmers, anti-big city reformers, and Nelson's job appointees—all funded with Chicago Board of Trade and James J. Hill money—were triumphant. William had been blind-sided. As the *Northwestern Miller* observed, "The option gamblers at Chicago were naturally elated over his defeat, as no man had ever given them harder battle. The railroad interests which find the Soo road an unpleasant competitor also got some consolation from Mr. Washburn's knock-out."[55]

The outcome was ironic, because both Washburn and Nelson had been born and raised on struggling farms with few advantages. Both had been enthusiastic Republicans in the Civil War. Both were energetic and ambitious. The differences emerged in their skills as politicians. William presumed his popularity and support; Nelson worked hard for every vote, as he had been doing for more than four years. Washburn's strength was among the power elite and king-makers of the party; Nelson's was among common people. Nelson loved a feisty campaign. The tall man in the castle at Fair Oaks distained to mix with scrappers. Though Washburn had done much for the state and city, he was somehow aloof from them. Nelson was Everyman.

---

55   *Northwestern Miller*, February 1, 1895.

Minnesota Historical Society
Norwegian-born Knute Nelson, a Union Army veteran, former congressman, governor, and four-term senator, defeated Washburn for reelection to the U.S. Senate in 1895.

While William Washburn had surpassed all his politician brothers, he did not match them as a political leader. He had the image, the aura, and the influence, but he was a poor vote-getter. Although he shared their personal honesty and ideals, William served in a time that had more to do with preserving things than changing them.

Brother Israel's record was marked by integrity, big goals, and eloquence. Unimpressive in appearance, little known outside the Penobscot District of Maine (a remote district in a remote state) and despite being rolled over by a clear majority in both houses of Congress, despite a contrary ruling by the Supreme Court, and despite opposition from two presidents, Israel led a political revolution in the country. Just 18 months after he suggested the name, his new Republican party swept every available office in Maine in 1856. The party went on to win the presidency just four years later.

Brother Elihu was equally honest, equally determined to stop the spread of slavery, and equally able to face great odds. He nurtured the Republican Party in Illinois and played a critical role in the war behind the scenes, where his victories had enormous consequences but left few paper records. As Israel persuaded Hannibal Hamlin, Lincoln's eventual vice president, to become a Republican in 1856, so Elihu probably influenced his friend Lincoln to become a Republican in 1858. Elihu spotted the military talent of a scruffy-looking constituent named Ulysses Grant, saw to it that he got command of the Union invasion force in Kentucky, twice saved him from being removed, and finally persuaded Lincoln to appoint him commander of the Union armies—thus insuring a commander who would win. In addition, again well out of the public eye, Elihu saw to it that dozens of incompetent or dishonest commanders were replaced—including his own party's first presidential candidate, John C. Fremont. Elihu also directed Grant's winning campaign for the presidency in 1868.

As young William was raising "Wide-Awake" volunteers for the Republicans in Minneapolis, his brother Charles was generating enthusiasm for the new party through rallies and sulfurous newspaper columns in California. Even blunt-talking brother Cadwallader—whose political skills may have been the worst in the family—played a steady part in the economic development of western Wisconsin, fought to curb the excesses of Milwaukee and Chicago railroad barons, stoutly resisted last-minute compromises to avoid civil war, and left a record of principled leadership in Congress and the governor's mansion of Wisconsin.

Except for William's success with the Mississippi River reservoir system, it is hard to find a contribution of comparable significance to these of his brothers. He was not part of a crusade like they were. Politically, William might have done better in the old world of France or England, rather than in the new world of the Upper Midwest. His successes in finding financing in London to save the Soo Line in 1886, and in later persuading the British to buy Pillsbury-Washburn in 1889, are evidence of his effectiveness in the Old World, where there were fewer calloused hands and sunburned faces in position to run things.

Although Knute Nelson would comfortably win reelection to the U.S. Senate three more times—finally winning endorsement from that last bastion of vengeful Washburn supporters, the Hennepin County Republican convention—William would have one more brief moment in the political spotlight. In 1900, supporters started beating the drum for him as a favorite-son candidate for the vice presidency. The *Minneapolis Journal* called his prospects "good," but the *Northwestern Miller* accurately doubted his chances, observing that "while he is a statesman, he is not a politician in the ordinary meaning of the word and has always been outspoken and frank in the expression of his opinions regardless of political effect."[56]

His old friends Thomas Lowry and Clinton Morrison went to the Republican national convention early that year in order to lay groundwork. Even Senator Nelson gave him an enthusiastic endorsement. But after 10 days or so of heady publicity, William graciously declined the consideration in favor of his friend Theodore Roosevelt. Roosevelt won the nomination and went on to conduct a wildly popular campaign for William McKinley, who won (over William Jennings Bryan) for a second time. When McKinley was assassinated, Roosevelt became president. By the end of the year, William said he was out of politics.[57]

What if William had won that nomination? It is hard to imagine him running the kind of popular campaign that Roosevelt did—although he had Roosevelt's vigor—let alone campaigning for the progressive causes championed by Roosevelt after he became president. William would never have challenged the Republican establishment. He had none of Roosevelt's charisma, military flair, or international experience. He disliked campaigning. He might have cost McKinley the election, for McKinley himself disliked campaigning.

---

56   *Northwestern Miller,* May 30, 1900; *Minneapolis Journal,* June 12, 1900.

57   *Minneapolis Journal,* December 5, 1900.

After the disastrous vote in January 1895 in St. Paul, Washburn took to his bed again at Fair Oaks. He would be called "Senator" for the rest of his life, and although his name would never again appear on a ballot, it would appear in print. In April 1903, for example, under the headline "Heads Off Tyranny," Senator Washburn was quoted by the faithful *Journal* expressing delight that James J. Hill's railroad consolidation scheme had been shot down by the U.S. Supreme Court in the Northern Securities case. "I haven't had anything please me so much in years," he told his interviewer.[58]

His political life was over, but he was far from finished with living.

---

[58] *Minneapolis Journal*, April 13, 1903.

7

Living Large
1859–1909

Like stately butterflies, the ladies moved up and down the impressive garden. Mr. Cleveland's graceful design was at last complete, and the glorious variety and colors in each flower bed drew forth a chorus of admiration as the troop in silk and muslin passed by. Lizzie Muzzy Washburn proudly led the way. The procession paused at the footbridge over an ornamental pond and looked back past the fountain, the greenhouse, and the stable toward the main house. In all the short history of Minneapolis, there had never been such an estate. These 10 acres of grounds, in the most desirable section of the city, had been a decade in planning and building. Lizzie had been involved in every step. How could Lizzie or William know that Fair Oaks, the mansion that loomed behind them, would not last much longer than its current occupants? Only the gardens would live on to be appreciated by later generations of Minneapolitans.[59]

⌁

Fair Oaks, the William Washburn family's house and gardens completed in 1883 from the design of E. Townshend Mix, was a grander estate than anything seen before in Minneapolis. Senator Washburn's stone palace was an 80-room extravaganza that dwarfed the homes of its staid Yankee neighbors. Battlements of Kasota stone were topped by a steep slate roof, interrupted by dozens of dormer windows, stepped gables, bays, and tall chimneys. A separate building housed coal bins and boilers that provided hot water and heated the home that was said to require a ton of coal a week in winter. Hundreds of tall, narrow windows

---

[59] Horace W. S. Cleveland was a Chicago landscape designer who prepared plans for the park systems of St. Paul and Minneapolis, the Washburn Park residential neighborhood, and the campus of the University of Minnesota.

The pool and fountain at Fair Oaks, William Washburn's Minneapolis estate, as featured on a 1910 postcard.

hinted at the high ceilings within and led viewers' eyes up to an enormous central tower, topped by a lightning rod at least 70 feet above ground level. That tower was visible across town. Huge stone porticoes and porches graced three sides of the building. At the main entrance, a curving drive led a high porte-cochere over a grand staircase and up to a pair of massive mahogany doors and a towering entrance hall.

Fair Oaks reflected the current status of its owner. There was little here to speak of the spectacular ups and downs of his life and nothing to indicate his humble origins back in Maine. The place spoke permanence and establishment. If ever Minneapolis had royalty, William Drew Washburn wanted the city to know that he was it.

William Washburn's life in the house resembled his life in business and politics. It was full of spectacular highs and dismal lows and lived at top speed. It was driven by exuberance, within a frame of image and propriety. It was, Lizzie would have admitted, never boring.

The castle at Fair Oaks aptly reflected the opulence of the Gilded Age and provided a showcase for its flamboyant owner.

Lizzie had joined William in Minneapolis in 1859. After spending her first three months in the drafty and noisy Nicollet House, the newlyweds got their first house. It was a rental—$15 a month—and Lizzie had to clean out chicken feathers before they could move in. They planted a garden and kept an eye out for animals such as foxes that stole their vegetables. On at least one occasion, the couple had to stand aside while a bear decimated their sweet corn.

They started a family almost immediately. When William was appointed surveyor general in 1861, they moved to St. Paul, where their first child was born— named Franklin, after Lizzie's father. Two years later their second boy, William Drew, Jr., came along.

A Universalist in faith, William joined other Mainers in town to establish a congregation. He chaired their first meeting and was elected to its board of trustees. In 1866 they built their first church at Fifth Street and Fourth Avenue. William gave the church its first organ, which a local newspaper called "the finest organ in the Northwest."[60] The congregation selected William's cousin Dorilus Morrison, the first mayor of Minneapolis (known to the Washburns as "Dory"), as chairman of the trustees, a position Morrison held until his death.

Ten years later in 1876, the parish built a fine stone church to replace their first building. William, a trustee again, contributed chimes and a bell tower for the new building.

Minnesota Historical Society

Minneapolis's Church of the Redeemer, in 1905, for which William Washburn donated a bell tower, the carillon it contained, and an enormous organ that filled the rear wall of the chancel.

It was a grand gesture—the first of many that William would make in the city. Not only did the bell tower's distinctive 212-foot height make the building known all over town as "the toothpick church," but for the next 20 years William's bells were probably the only ones in the city. In 1888, when the Church of the Redeemer burned, the great tower survived the fire. William's contribution to the replacement building, completed not

60   Rev. Marion D. Shutter, from a history of the church included in fiftieth anniversary book, December 12, 1909.

long after he was elected to the U.S. Senate in 1889, was a spectacular organ. It was set amid carvings by the first Kaiser Wilhelm's personal sculptor, a man named Pelzer, whom William probably met during one of his sojourns in Germany.

Over the years, Washburn had many business associates in the congregation with him, including Major Hale, Charles M. Loring, Paris Gibson, Thomas Lowry and cousin Dory's son, Clinton Morrison. Indeed, like his old Passadumkeag Club, William's Universalist Church of the Redeemer was a power center of early Minneapolis.

William's church involvement was more than superficial. Following in the steps of his brother Israel, William achieved national stature within the Universalist denomination. He was named president of the Universalist Convention in Buffalo in 1881 and later served a two-year term as the national lay leader of the faith. In 1909, William was honored with a silver loving cup on the church's fiftieth anniversary.[61] This was also the year that young John Washburn—brother Sid's oldest son who became chairman of Washburn-Crosby Company—was elected to join his uncle on the church's board of trustees. Changes such as the election of a new trustee were big events in the conservative parish—during most of its first 50 years it had only two ministers.

William Washburn was also interested in education. He became a trustee of the Minneapolis Female Seminary in 1869, just before the first of his three years on the Minneapolis School Board. When the school became the Bennett Seminary, William served on its board for 30 more years. He also supported a public library for the community as early as 1859. When a handsome downtown library and athenaeum was constructed in 1885, William donated $5,000.

Almost as long as his association with the Church of the Redeemer was William's support for the orphanage that was his brother Cadwallader's great gift to the city of Minneapolis. After Cad's death in 1883, his will specified a bequest of more than $375,000 ($8.5 million today) and gave William the task of establishing the home. William, after helping obtain the land and getting an impressive building built, served

---

61 William's son Cadwallader later returned this cup to the church.

For nearly 30 years William Washburn made sure that his brother Cadwallader's greatest bequest to the city of Minneapolis, the Washburn Orphans Asylum, contributed to the community. Today it continues to serve 4,000 Minneapolis families a year as the Washburn Child Guidance Center.

with his sister Caroline on the board of trustees (with William as president) until their deaths three decades later. Over the years a galaxy of Martin, Hale, Pillsbury, Pray, Crosby, and Morrison family members also served on this board.

Many of William's activities forwarded the welfare of his adopted city. Besides the first association of businessmen, the first street car company, and the first electric light company, William worked to give Minneapolis a new city hall and court house. In 1870, with two partners, he had acquired a prime site, but his offer to a suspicious city council was declined by a single vote. Apparently any bad taste from this experience was dissipated by 1887, for he was made chairman that year of a special board of commissioners that selected a site and a design for a sumptuous new city headquarters.

As the city grew, so did William's family. The couple had more children: Cadwallader Lincoln, their third son, in 1866; Mary, their first girl, in 1868; and Edwin in 1870. With five young children the family determined to build their first house. They picked a site on the outskirts of Minneapolis—about a mile from the mills on the canal—but they were soon surrounded by other comfortable residences. Despite William's wide-ranging commercial and political activities, the couple would live in their Seventh Avenue house for the next 22 years. It was here that they would bring up the six surviving children of the nine born to them.

To help with the brood, they added a governess to the household. Ellen Brooks, born in New York, had married a man who had lost everything in the war and died. Although used to "the gentle life of the South," according to her obituary, Ellen would serve the Washburn family for 42 years until her death at the age of 80.[62] Very much a member of the family, she was buried in the Washburn plot at Lakewood Cemetery, which William had helped organize in 1871.

In that year the Washburn family suffered setbacks. Son Cadwallader Lincoln, age five, became deaf and speechless through concurrent attacks of meningitis and scarlet fever. The family promptly learned sign language. As his brother Stanley later reported, Cadwallader never thought it a handicap, just "sometimes an inconvenience." Lizzie bore another boy, George, who died after six weeks, and then a second daughter, Elizabeth, in 1874.

While William's own family was growing rapidly, he did not forget about his siblings' families. He took in his closest sister Caroline, widowed in the Civil War with two small children and, with brother Cadwallader's help, built a modest house for her in 1870, where she lived for the next 50 years.

William also offered a roof and protection for one of his brother Israel's children, a troubled son named Charles Fox Washburn. Charles died in 1884, only a year after his father. In 1886, William stepped in to pay $2,800 to take care of at least one of the young man's unpaid obligations in Minnesota.[63]

---

62 Her death was noted in an unidentified clipping in Washburn Library, probably from a Minneapolis paper.

63 *Fergus Falls Journal*, May 15, 1886.

The year after William's daughter Elizabeth was born, the family took its first grand excursion to Europe. The trip might have been designed by brother Elihu to get William away from his creditors in the wake of the 1873 economic crash, or it might have been William's own idea to show those same creditors that he wasn't worried, and they shouldn't be either. In Paris William's entourage met Elihu and his family before proceeding to Cannes for several weeks on the Riviera. From there the two brothers made a solo expedition to Egypt to rub elbows with Ferdinand de Lesseps at the newly-opened Suez Canal. William also

Exporail, Canadian Railway Museum

Private rail cars provided mobile command centers for railroad moguls, as well as impressive symbols of their owner's status. This photo shows the interior of Van Horne's palace car "Saskatchewan," which replaced the "Matapedia" after it was wrecked by a rock slide in British Columbia.

discovered the recuperative powers of the baths at Carlsbad, which he continued to visit each year for the rest of his life.[64]

William loved conducting entourages. His long involvement with railroading gave him access to private railroad cars on associated lines as well as on his own lines. As the family grew, he had no trouble filling up cars, astounding locals wherever he arrived and departed. After he and his brothers completed a mansion for his nearly-blind father on the old Maine farmstead in 1868, William arrived with his family at the nearby Livermore Falls station almost every summer for the next 40 years. It must

---

64   The mineral springs at Carlsbad in Bohemia (part of the Austro-Hungarian empire in William's time and now the Czech Republic) have been famous for their curative value since the thirteenth century.

have required the assistance of all the livery drivers within miles to transport the family, servants, and trunks several miles up to Norlands (named by his brother Charles after a Tennyson poem in 1869).

On one Maine vacation the family suffered an unexpected tragedy. Oldest son Frank drowned in a swimming accident while the family was vacationing at Scarborough Beach in 1877. William's ebullience must have been tempered for some time, but Lizzie delivered another boy, Stanley, the following year. A daughter, Alice, died a month after her birth in 1881. In all, William and Lizzie saw six children, four boys and two girls, grow to maturity—first in their busy house on Seventh Street and later in the castle at Fair Oaks.

No matter where they lived, the Washburn home was a decidedly busy place. There were, of course, servants, including nurses, housemaids, and cooks inside and grooms and gardeners outside. The children had house pets and ponies and horses in the stables. A stream of visitors from William's political and commercial enterprises passed through the house, and the family entertained often and well.

Lizzie had many opportunities to visit with her family back in Bangor. When her sister Olive married Bangor entrepreneur John Crosby, whom Cadwallader Washburn invited to help manage his Minneapolis flour mill in 1877, the sisters must have been delighted at the opportunity to share their lives. Despite the sometimes strained relationship between Washburn and John Crosby, the Crosby and Washburn cousins were close.

Given William's outspoken nature at home, which his children seem to have inherited, the family atmosphere was probably loud and tumultuous. Youngest son Stanley, who became a well known newspaper reporter, recalled, "From my earliest recollections, our household was constantly in a state of chaos and confusion."[65] Stanley also remembered that his father "insisted that the family accompany him on his many travels. I was age two at the Republican convention in Chicago when Garfield was nominated." (He was too young to remember that this was the same convention that almost nominated his uncle Elihu instead.)

Stanley, bed-ridden with scarlet fever when his father was first elected to Congress, recalled the family move to Washington, D.C.: "The horses,

---

65 Stanley Washburn, Sr., unpublished autobiography, 6–7, Washburn Papers.

servants, chickens, and rabbits . . . had already gone, so I was wrapped up and placed in a private (railroad) car for the long trek to the capitol." They took a large house on I Street, where, Stanley wrote, the atmosphere was the same as it had been in Minneapolis: "The house was constantly filled with politicians, from congressmen to members of the cabinet. Here too chaos and confusion prevailed."

After William completed the castle at Fair Oaks, construction of the Soo railroad "brought more bedlam, with railroad men, contractors, engineers, and all the back-wash of railroad construction filling the house day and night." When the Grand Army of the Republic had their national convention in Minneapolis, Stanley remembered that four different Civil War generals stayed at their house —Logan, Fairchild, Sickles, and Chamberlain.

Stanley also reflected that not everything at the new mansion was a success. One of its innovations was an elevator run by water. Unfortunately, the contraption used so much water that it emptied the mansion's only water tank after a couple of trips. It took two hours of hand pumping to refill the tank. The elevator, he reported, was abandoned.

Well-educated himself, William did not skimp on his children's education. William, Jr., graduated from Yale in 1888, the same year Mary graduated from the Ogontz School in Pennsylvania. Her brother Cadwallader graduated from Gallaudet in 1890 and Massachusetts Institute of Technology in 1893. Edwin went off to Yale in 1891, Elizabeth to Radcliffe the following year, and Stanley to Hill School and then Williams College, graduating in 1901.

Through all the comings and goings, Lizzie somehow retained her poise. A gracious hostess, she oversaw the staff of servants that ran the great household—wherever it happened to be. When her children became as peripatetic as her husband, this became more difficult. Stanley, sounding as pleased with himself as his father, observed that his mother "seemed always bewildered by the meteor-like swiftness of her son's tumultuous life." Given the number of meteors around her, this was understandable.

Lizzie left no more records than her husband William. Other than reminiscences about her early years as told by her daughter Mary—a narrative that ends with Lizzie's first year in Minneapolis—very little

The faithful *Minneapolis Journal* covered launching of the lake cruiser *Minneapolis* in 1891.

remains from her more than 60 years in the city. What happened to her relations with her sister when Olive's husband John Crosby fired William in 1879? What happened when Crosby was forced to take William back in 1883, and was there any link felt between Washburn's presence and Crosby's death in 1887? No written records give clues.

One surviving story recounted in James Gray's history of General Mills suggests the level of intensity in the Washburn household. "Surrounded by his four sons and two daughters, all as opinionated as himself," Gray wrote, "Washburn would dominate their discussion even as its crescendo of challenge and defiance grew higher and higher." Because young Cadwallader was deaf, "a handicap which with characteristic Washburn determination he refused to acknowledge," Cad would ask "at the peak of a family wrangle . . . by sign language, to be told what the argument was about. It would then begin all over again at the tips of flying fingers. To conclude the matter, the senator would refer the point at issue to the encyclopedia, and if this authority failed to sustain his own opinion, he disdainfully hurled the corpulent volume across the room."[66] One wonders what Lizzie thought or did. Was she "bewildered"—the word Stanley used—or did she jump right in with the rest of the family?

Washburn Library

The Washburn mansion at Livermore, Maine, was the scene of regular family visits for many decades.

Stanley, age nine in 1889 when the family moved back to Washington for his father's term as senator, remembered conferences going on "hour after hour" between senate colleagues and cabinet members. He specifically remembered Secretary of State James G. Blaine, as well as Senators Aldrich (from Rhode Island) and Allison (from Iowa), and the gigantic speaker of the house, Thomas B. Reed (from Maine). Stanley called these discussions "all the intrigues of that class of men in politics."

Washington family activities even included a ship's christening— the Navy cruiser U.S.S. *Minneapolis*—by Stanley's sister Elizabeth, age 19. The *Minneapolis Journal* devoted much of its front page to the occasion— including the story of William's long effort to have the vessel named after his home town and an artist's sketch of a very no-nonsense looking young Elizabeth Washburn.[67] One wonders if William would have been pleased at the Navy's description of the new ship as a "commerce destroyer."

After Congress adjourned, summers provided occasions for regular family trips to Maine and junkets to Europe. Stanley went abroad in 1889, first to the baths at Carlsbad and then—for Lizzie, the two girls, and Stanley—a winter in Berlin. They returned to Minneapolis in March 1890.

Trips to Maine were grand affairs, especially after 1890. By this time, William was the last surviving brother of the original seven, and he steadily added field and forest land to the property around the Livermore farm. He bought neighboring properties for his two daughters and son

---

66 Gray, *General Mills*, 14.

67 *Minneapolis Journal*, August 12, 1893.

Cadwallader, and he expanded the original farm's acreage, even cutting carriage trails through the woods. He entertained a steady stream of guests, and summer evenings on the great porch were filled with loud talk and cigar smoke.

Despite the fact that he had been born and raised in Livermore, William made little effort to interact with local residents there. He had joined with his brothers to pay for a new library and refurbish the church for the community as much as for the family. Now, with his brothers gone, William entertained summer houseguests in isolation from the community. Like an old-world barony— and unlike his party-going peers at summer colonies in Newport and Saratoga—the seigneur chose to stay at the Norlands estate, a grand and isolated summer refuge.

The one exception to this routine related to his love of speed and fast horses. In Minneapolis the Washburns were known for the immaculate glass-fronted landau and the extended-front brougham that carried them around town, their large pair of bang-tailed bay horses, and the green livery of their coach drivers.[68] The sleepy roads in back-country Maine provided an opportunity for William to break out of this staid respectability. There was nothing William loved to do more in Livermore than hitch a team of good horses to the best buggy and go for a drive. He usually drove alone, for the reason that nobody else had the nerve to go with him. These trips along the narrow dirt roads were done at top speed—which did not endear William to the locals.

One story describes William coming upon elderly milkman Frank Partridge, weary after a day of going from farm to farm picking up heavy cans of cream for the local creamery. It was springtime—in Maine called "Mud Season." The only solid path on the gravel road was down the two narrow tracks in the center of the road. Partridge's daughter Beatrice reported hearing that "the inevitable happened. Mr. Partridge was near the end of his route with a heavy load. If he had to turn aside from the center, his heavy wagon would be hopelessly mired. But trotting merrily along toward him in the road center was William Drew in his buggy. The two teams met nose to nose in the center. William stood up in his vehicle and yelled, 'I guess you don't know who I am!' To which Mr. Partridge replied, 'I thought you wuz God

---

68   *St. Paul Daily Globe*, July 19, 1887.

Almighty the way you was acting!' . . . Washburn got his come-uppance. He sot down, backed up his vehicle to a turn-out spot, and let old Mr. Partridge pass."[69]

In 1892, thanks to William, the national Republican Party held its national convention in Minneapolis. Fourteen-year-old Stanley was allowed to return from his eastern prep school for the gala event, probably Fair Oaks' finest hour. No less than three past and future presidents, as well as 18 congressional guests, visited. (Stanley himself gave up his room for Ohio's William McKinley.) Stanley's father, who favored James G.

Maine Historical Society

An 1889 cartoon in the magazine *Puck* implied that Blaine was once again eyeing the presidency

Blaine for the nomination, had 6,000 Blaine posters hidden in a vault in the basement. When Blaine failed to get the nomination, young Stanley was so upset that he returned to Fair Oaks from the convention hall and lowered the mansion's five enormous American flags to half mast. William was not pleased, and young Stanley heard about this for the next 20 years from his father and from the former guests. The flag incident did bring about a rare moment of intimacy between the two, and William talked to Stanley "quite confidentially for a long time—which was unusual," Stanley said, because "he almost never discussed serious subjects with his children."

Washburn family events and entourages began to include children marrying. In 1890, oldest son William married Florence Savier in

---

69   Ethel (Billie) Gammon, "Still No Flies on Bill," unpublished manuscript , in possession of Cinda Foster, Livermore, Maine.

Portland, Oregon. Two years later, Fair Oaks saw its first wedding, when Mary married Elbert Baldwin, a magazine editor in New York City. For this epic event William spared no expense. According to one account, no less than 3,000 invitations were sent out.[70] Edwin followed, marrying Ethel Fraser in New Jersey, where they settled.

William Washburn's defeat for reelection to the Senate in 1895 led to an unexpected change of pace. In 1896 he received a communication from William C. Van Horne, the Canadian Pacific boss of the Soo Line. Van Horne informed William that a man with power and influence in the emperor of China's court was seeking someone to build a railroad and that he would be traveling on a special Canadian Pacific train through Winnipeg.

William had his own car taken to Canada and attached to the train of visitor Li Hung Chang. Their rolling discussion went well, and William was subsequently invited to visit the emperor. In December 1896 he undertook his biggest trip yet— across the Pacific to China. Accompanying him was an entourage that included Lizzy, daughter Elizabeth, son Stanley, his niece Maud (Israel's daughter), a lawyer, a banker, a mining expert, and his old engineering colleague from the Soo Line, Capt. Watson W. Rich. Washburn spent several months enduring palace intrigues about this possible construction of a railroad from Peking to Hankow.[71]

When Li Hung Chang fell out of power, however, William had to give up on the scheme, but the trip had some unexpected consequences. On the long voyage across the Pacific, Elizabeth was courted by the ship's doctor, Englishman Hamilton Wright, whom she married in a huge ceremony at Fair Oaks in 1899 before settling in Kuala Lumpur. At a party in Peking, William's son Stanley also met his future wife, Alice Langhorne, whom he married in Washington, D.C., nine years later. Lizzie Washburn was so taken with the architecture of pagodas that she supposedly persuaded William to incorporate one into a railroad station built in North Dakota shortly after they returned.

---

70   *Delano Eagle*, December 15, 1892.

71   Much correspondence exists concerning this effort in William Drew Washburn's file, Washburn Family Papers.

When the Washburns left China, they traveled westward through Russia, where William was personally thanked by the czar for helping provide flour for southern Russia four years earlier. He thus became the second son of one poor Maine farmer to be thanked for his services by crowned heads of Europe. (His brother Elihu had been thanked by the French and Prussians for his services in Paris.)

Ironically, the one member of the excursion to China who experienced commercial success was Captain Rich. He was quietly commissioned to do a preliminary survey of the thousand-mile route from Peking to Hankow, which he carried out with his customary efficiency in the face of delays and intrigues. Afterwards he was retained in the employ of the railroad, and he moved with his wife and three children to Shanghai, where he died in 1903.

Back in Minneapolis, Elizabeth's marriage to Dr. Wright provided a fresh opportunity to show off Fair Oaks. A newspaper report of the wedding ceremony spoke of "beautiful appointments" and a "brilliant gathering." The library was converted into a chapel, and a pipe organ was brought in. The bridal procession—made up of four Washburns and two Crosbys—moved down the grand staircase between tall palms and drooping ferns and clouds of flowers. Stanley acted as best man for the groom. The concluding banquet was served around a mound of orchids between silver and gold candelabra. Afterwards, the couple left for New York in F. D. Underwood's private railroad car, on their way to join artist brother Cadwallader in France and thence to India and Kuala Lumpur.[72]

Mother-of-the-bride Lizzie Washburn was justifiably proud of the interior of Fair Oaks. She had planned every detail, including massive carved doors of Spanish mahogany and heavy bronze fixtures opening onto a vestibule with a mosaic marble floor bearing William's monogram. An inner vestibule was finished in Circassian walnut. Adjoining the vestibule was a great hall—the east end furnished in mahogany and the west end in oak. Other first-floor rooms included a library, sitting room, smoking room, conservatory, and drawing room. Fireplaces were onyx and marble, with mosaic hearthstones. All these rooms boasted huge carpets and ornate

---

72   Minneapolis *Journal*, November 28, 1899.

Northwestern Miller, *December 1884,*
Hennepin County Library

William allowed an artist to make
sketches of the Fair Oaks mansion's
exterior and interior in 1894.

ceilings. A large dining room, with butler's pantry, featured inlaid maple
floors, stained glass windows, large chandeliers, and walls covered in fine
fabric. Abundant green plants included pine trees at Christmastime and
potted tropical palms and ferns, which must have been a challenge to
maintain in Minneapolis in January—even with a furnace that consumed a
ton of coal a week and the assistance of gardeners and a large greenhouse.
Other notable elements of the decor in 1899 included a Chinese Buddha
sculpture and an enormous bearskin rug. William's office, billiard room,
the couple's bedroom, Lizzie's boudoir, a sewing room, and many, many
guest bedrooms and baths filled the second floor.[73]

One can almost picture William at Fair Oaks on December 23, 1902,
presiding over the annual dinner he threw for the Bowdoin Association of
Minnesota. Of course, he was president of the group—the *Journal* called
him "the dean" of the association.[74] It is easy to imagine him at the head of
the long dinner table, basking in the toasts of his admiring guests. His alma

---

73   The servant's quarters and kitchen were not mentioned in the reporter's
     glowing article in the *Northwestern Miller* in December 1884, though he did
     mention the view from the tower as "unsurpassed."

74   *Minneapolis Journal*, December 24, 1902.

mater had awarded him an honorary Doctor of Laws degree the previous June, so he could now be called "Doctor," as well as "Senator" and "General."

No event showed off Fair Oaks more than the Washburns' annual New Year's Eve parties. Every window in the great home shone with light and grounds and stables filled with horse-drawn coaches brining the elites of Minneapolis and St. Paul. Music offered up by a full orchestra echoed from the mansion in the frosty night air. A published guest list from the event in 1908 listed three hundred guests, including Crosbys and Bells, Pillsburys and Hills, Morrisons and Lowrys, Christians and Martins, Lorings and Hales. Whatever run-ins might have occurred in the past, all was forgotten in the warm glow of that annual party. Resplendent in formal wear, Senator and Mrs. Washburn held court at Fair Oaks, and a staff of more than 40 servants made sure that food and libation flowed. The elite of both cities turned out to honor—and be honored by—the family that had been prominent so long.[75]

Three of Washburn's six children were in town to take their places in the family reception line at the 1908 bash. They were a colorful group in their own right. William, Jr., who had returned to Minneapolis, was elected to the state legislature for 16 straight years. Cadwallader Lincoln, with a solid reputation as an artist, was there on his way to pursue his art in Mexico—with some freelance work for newspapers on the side. Edwin was also present, although he resided in New Jersey and held an important position with the Baltimore and Ohio Railroad in New York. Stanley, home after several years of adventuring around the world, was helping his brother William wind down the steel company William, Sr., had organized to manufacture the railroad couplers that his brother Edwin had invented. Only sisters Mary and Elizabeth were absent, both overseas.

As the partygoers kept the lights burning at Fair Oaks burning into the night on New Year's Eve, the head of the household had every reason to mirror the carefree exuberance of his children. William Drew Washburn was flying high.

---

75   The 1908 guest list is interesting for the names that were not on it. The absence of political and immigrant names emphasizes William's preference for a social circle quite separate from the new forces in the state. His standing in this circle would have been severely tested by the events of 1909.

8

Flying Higher
1882–1908

The railroad siding sat in a vast yellow plain. Next to the rails huddled a few shacks, and lonely box cars gave the wind something to whistle through. Emptiness stretched to the horizon in every direction, with only an occasional tree dotting the sea of grass. A hot wind whistled in the ears of the people gathered by the rails.

In the center of the crowd, a tall figure gesticulated. Probably the best-dressed man in North Dakota that day, he held a roll of blueprints in his hands. Although 71 years old, he spoke with the enthusiasm and excitement of a much younger man. He would, he said, build a town here. It would be named "Wilton," after a town near where he had grown up. Wilton would have the largest lignite coal mine in the world—coal to power trains and heat buildings for four hundred miles around, all the way to Minneapolis. Hundreds of Norwegian immigrants would work here in the winter, when the bitter cold and snow suspended farming. He would build the Wilton railroad depot right here, with an apartment for himself on the second floor. It would look something like a Chinese pagoda. Here were the drawings—straight from the emperor's court in China. Fantastic though it might be, if William Washburn said it was going to happen, then it would happen. Almost everything else he had said would happen had happened. Why not Wilton, North Dakota?

As death began to take his siblings, William "Young Rapid" Washburn had lost little of the speed or energy that had delighted them on the farm in Livermore. Without letting up on his railroads, politics, and flour milling activities, he enthusiastically entered into a kaleidoscope of new projects—both to make profit or not.

In the late nineteenth century, the term "businessman" usually described someone who devoted his talent and energy to a single enterprise or a family of enterprises. William's brother Cadwallader was typical—bowing out of railroading in order to concentrate on milling. For William Drew Washburn, however, "business" meant taking on whatever caught his attention. And his attention was never still.

His son Stanley's description of the "bedlam" at Fair Oaks accurately

Minnesota Historical Society

When the Lincoln Mill burned in 1884, it took most of Anoka on the Mississippi River with it. Within 18 months, Washburn had a new mill in operation.

summed his father's life upon his return from Congress to Minneapolis in 1882. At the same time that William was putting together financing and construction for the three different railroads that would eventually become the Soo Line, he was also launching dozens of other projects with mind-boggling rapidity.

Granted, some were forced on him by circumstance. In 1884, for example, with his new railroad under construction east across Wisconsin and west toward the Dakota Territory, he opened up his big new flour mill in Anoka. When an enormous fire burned down much of Anoka—86 buildings in all—he had to immediately replace his destroyed Lincoln Flour Mill there.

William and his stalwart partner William Hale first had to handle the flood of grain already headed for Anoka. Since William's partner at the Palisade Mill in Minneapolis, Leonard Day, had just died, Washburn was able to buy Day's interest and handle the Lincoln orders there. In fact, Washburn then centralized administration of all three of his mills by incorporating them under the umbrella of the Washburn Mill Company. By 1889, his total flour production reached about 2,800 barrels a day. This was only a quarter of the output of each of his rivals, C. A. Pillsbury and Washburn-Crosby, but it made him one of the major flour millers in town.

Orphan's Asylum from Minnesota Historical Society; others from Hennepin County Library

During the late 1880s, William Washburn was involved closely with four prominent new buildings in Minneapolis: the Washburn Orphan's Asylum, the Minneapolis City Hall, the Industrial Exposition Building, and the Minneapolis Harvester Works.

In Anoka at the same time, Washburn was also nursing along his new Anoka National Bank, which opened in August 1883 with himself as president. (The bank survived through various crises until 1931.) William had also extended his interest in Anoka with a new opera house. Although it also burned in 1884, he continued to buy real estate in the town for additional business use.

Back in Minneapolis, following up on their successful intervention with the North Star Woolen Mill, William partnered with the Morrisons to buy control of the ailing Minneapolis Harvester Works, an early venture to provide locally-made equipment to the region's farmers. Thanks to the invention of a new twine binder, the company quickly returned to profitability. William, who was not involved in daily operations, joined Dorilus and his son Clinton on the board until the company was sold in 1892. In another action, William

Minnesota Historical Society

For the Industrial Exposition of 1888, the Minnesota Brush Electric Company, of which William was an early investor, engineered a spectacular display of street lighting along Nicollet Avenue—the first of its kind in the country.

ended his partnership with George Newell in the grocery business, although Newell stayed involved with William on the Soo Line board through the financing crisis experienced in late 1886.

Parallel with his railroading adventures, William also engaged in major public service in his adopted city. Under his direction, two years of planning and preparation resulted in the Great Minneapolis Industrial Exposition, held in an impressive new exhibit hall amid great hoopla in August–September 1888. Through this ambitious project, Minneapolis was able to show itself off to the whole world. William's work to bring the Republican Party national convention there in 1892 helped further this effort.

William was good at hoopla. He helped supply a spectacular feature for the 1888 exposition along one of the city's main streets, Nicollet Avenue. New electrical street lighting, powered with electricity generated from the Falls of St. Anthony debuted at the industrial exposition. Providing the service was the fledgling Minnesota Brush Electric Company, in which William was a founding stockholder. No other city in the country could boast such lighting. No one was prouder of the display or surer of its business future than William.

There was more. William's offer to city fathers of an attractive plot of land for a new city hall had been declined in 1882, but five years later city leaders asked him to spearhead the effort to build a spectacular new combined courthouse and city hall. Although it took two years for planning and site preparation, and although it was not fully occupied until 1906, the building offered a new symbol of municipal pride. Soaring above the massive copper roof, its bell tower was larger than London's fabled Big Ben. Ten huge bells (later, 15 bells) provided noontime concerts starting in 1896.

In addition to his business and civic contributions, William was also involved in real estate projects. One of these was an elite residential development along Minnehaha Creek. As William completed his own castle at Fair Oaks, he joined with several others to start an exclusive enclave on 220 acres named Washburn Park. In this same area, he set aside 20 acres for the Washburn Memorial Orphan Asylum, his brother Cadwallader's bequest to the city. Under William's direction, the construction of a large residential complex for housing and training orphan children, including a dairy farm, was completed on this site. It was dedicated in June 1887, and William chaired its board for the rest of his life.

Amid all of this activity, William continued to meet responsibilities related to the original source of his fortune. Working with the competent and reliable Major Hale, William devoted time to milling matters almost every day. New orders coming in from overseas required new levels of production for both farmers and millers—and kept Fair Oaks afloat. But this same prosperity meant new commitments to deliver products half way around the world at contracted prices.

If the supply was scare, sometimes extraordinary efforts were required to obtain it. In the dead of the winter of 1887, with his railroad, civic, and political activities at full speed, William was reported on the ground in remote Hankinson, North Dakota, personally bidding 80 cents a bushel for No. 1 hard wheat, more than was being paid for it in Minneapolis.[76]

Variables affecting his mills' annual production included the size of the annual grain harvest, the cost and speed of transportation—from the

---

76   *Richland County Gazette*, February 25, 1887.

fields to the mills, and from the mills to the buyers—and the fragile nature of the mills themselves. Mills could blow up or burn down. The Great Plains had droughts, locusts arrived, waterpower varied with the seasons, railroad rates fluctuated, and angry farmers forced unrealistic laws through the legislature.[77] Dozens of factors could get in the way of a miller's contracted obligation to deliver his product to a certain place by a certain time.

Washburn learned this firsthand when he decided to enter the wheat farming business. Like his rival James J. Hill, he purchased and operated several wheat farms of his own, but he quickly realized the vagaries of summer weather. In 1886, he lost 700 acres of wheat in just one summer storm. Some neighbors were hit even harder. Moved by their plight, he shipped carloads of provisions and blankets to his Normandy Farm near Willmar, Minnesota, to help neighbors wiped out by this same storm.[78]

As the size of orders for flour in Minneapolis steadily increased, flour millers' businesses became more and more of a balancing act. As with any commodity, the price of grain was directly affected by how much of it there was at any given time as well as how much the market needed. Both could fluctuate wildly. Flour prices declined from 1883 to 1887, then zoomed up in 1888. The major players were buying and selling by contract. By the end of the decade, most flour milling in Minneapolis was being done by just four mills, with C. A. Pillsbury and Washburn-Crosby dominating. The biggest mills had the most to lose, and it was not surprising that as the 1880s came to a close, operators like Charles Pillsbury were wearying of the game that they had kept going for so long.

William was not immune to these pressures, and he continued regular personal vacations to Maine and Europe to recuperate. This enthusiasm for the larger world was not necessarily endorsed by most Minnesotans, however, and many were suspicious and resentful of the "outside" forces upon which so many major businesses came to depend. As early as 1882, Minnesotans had great pride in the local ownership of the Minneapolis

---

77   Gray, *General Mills*, 20, reported that the explosion of 1878 had, with one stroke, removed one half of the city's flour production.

78   *Willmar Republican Gazette*, December 30, 1886. Normandy Farm was located in the township of Edwards, about 15 miles southwest of Willmar.

and St. Louis Railroad and felt great dismay when its control slipped into the hands of New York bankers and then to Chicago railroad men. As international orders rolled in to the flour mills by the falls, ambivalence grew. Farmers and millers welcomed the new business, but city journalists expressed their wariness about the influence of new outsider buyers.[79]

In 1888 new players showed up on the flour-milling scene. Straight from London, England, a small team of agents arrived in Minneapolis with lust in their eyes. The millers' profits had caught their attention from halfway around the world. So had the potential for new sales in Europe, where buyers were just now becoming aware of the superiority of Minnesota's product. These men were interested in acquiring the mills, and they had deep pockets. They had authorization to spend more money than local millers believed possible.

Both the Pillsburys and William Washburn proved open to offers. Charles A. Pillsbury was tired of constant pressure, and William would consider almost any scheme that would allow him to try other things. His brother Cadwallader was gone, and his successors at Washburn-Crosby, who had won control from Washburn family heirs, had immediately fired William again. These new men were determined to retain the independence for which they had worked so hard. (The Washburn-Crosby firm in fact would survive as an independent entity until it became General Mills 25 years later.)

William's own flour milling operations were flourishing, and he still controlled the waterpower on the west bank of the falls. His lumber mill in Anoka had survived the 1884 fire and continued its enormous production of lumber, shingles and laths until it burned in another fire in 1887. Because the pinelands along the Rum River were nearly gone by this time, and perhaps with Major Hale's urging, William decided not to rebuild this enterprise.

Instead, William took a bold step in another direction. He approached the Pillsburys about merging all their flour mills and waterpower companies and then selling the whole package to the British. Maybe, he

---

79 Hofsommer, *Minneapolis and the Age of Railways*, 103, includes quotes from the *Minneapolis Tribune* from 1877 through 1883, including comments by the Minnesota Railroad Commissioner about the Minneapolis and St. Louis falling under the control of Chicago interests.

Minnesota Historical Society

The river bank behind these loggers on the Rum River in 1900 suggests the approaching depletion of the white and red pine forest in Minnesota.

thought, British owners would even allow them to continue the management of their operations. It was a complex proposal, but the Pillsburys said they were interested.

Negotiations lasted for months. At last, in 1889 the deal was done. The merger and sale were accomplished. A new entity, Pillsbury-Washburn Flour Mills Company Ltd., was organized in England, but responsibility for its operation was placed with an American management committee that included both William and the Pillsburys. The British got ownership and nominal control—albeit from a very great distance. The Americans got lots of money, plus continued on-the-spot operating responsibility. William's share of the profit from the sale was more than $1.5 million in 1889 dollars. This was by far his biggest business triumph.

During the 1890s two more efforts by outsiders to capture the flour-milling industry would give more credence to Minnesotans' fears of outside control. Chicago speculator Joseph Leiter was defeated in his effort to corner the wheat market only by the huge size of the 1898 crop, which lowered prices and forced Leiter to liquidate his holdings. More serious was an effort in 1899 by New York promoter Thomas A. McIntyre to unite all of the country's flour mills into a gigantic trust. The McIntyre effort was defeated only when local investors quietly bought enough stock to retain stockholder control of the Washburn and the Pillsbury mills and when the millers elected to purchase rather than lease their buildings. As the *Northwest Miller* proudly crowed, "Mr. McIntyre may purchase other mills elsewhere . . . but without one or more of the three large Minneapolis plants now entirely out of his reach, he can do nothing in the nature of a flour trust, and from this great and threatening danger, the entire industry has been happily rescued."[80]

There was no question that the British were serious about their new acquisition. New capital came rolling in to Pillsbury-Washburn that permitted major improvements in the existing mills and construction of new facilities, as well.

For William, this sale meant a comfortable prolongation of his lavish lifestyle—a continuing procession of guests at Fair Oaks, yearly European sojourns at the Carlsbad baths (in part to contend with a large gain in weight), and more entourages to dazzle the locals from Maine to Moscow. (This was not without hazard. In 1895 William and his family were on a fishing trip when their train derailed near Elbow Lake and their private car was flipped into a ditch at high speed. They all escaped serious injury from flying furniture, but the car was demolished.)[81]

The British sale also opened the door to still more enterprises. While most people might have quietly retreated behind their mansion doors to a respectable retirement, not Young Rapid.

North Dakota, which gained statehood in 1889, offered rich potential for growing wheat, and over the next 10 years the land along the Upper Missouri River north of Bismarck became the next undeveloped breadbasket area attracting armies of settlers. New towns formed across the flat grasslands, including one near the old site of Fort Mandan. Its founders, Wisconsin natives, named it Washburn after Cadwallader, who they had admired as governor of that state.

---

80 *Northwestern Miller*, April 12, 1899, p. 687.

81 *Grant County Herald*, September 12, 1895.

New towns erupted quickly on the empty prairies of the Dakotas: an aerial view showing materials being unloaded for a town around 1908 at Hettinger, North Dakota, and William Washburn's finished settlement of Langhorn.

William himself bought farm land there and then organized investors to build yet another railroad. In 1899, the Bismarck, Washburn, and Fort Buford Railroad was incorporated to build up the east side of the Missouri River north of Bismarck. Once again, William was president. For the next five years, through dust storms to howling blizzards, William's rails crept north. The company grew to include two steamboats, named *Washburn* and *Expansion*, and the first grain barges on the Upper Missouri River. Before the line was sold to the Soo Line in 1904, the company, renamed the Bismarck, Washburn, and Great Falls Railroad, also owned a hotel.

Construction crews building the grade for the new railroad brought Washburn's attention to yet another opportunity. While cutting through some low hills, they uncovered rich seams of lignite coal. Since the winters were cold and heating material was scarce, lignite could fill the need for inexpensive fuel to heat homes and fire up steam engines. The coal that William had been getting from Iowa was petering out, and demand from across the Midwest—including the Soo Line's need to power its locomotives and heat hundreds of remote station houses—was increasing. While lignite produced only about 65 percent of the heat of eastern coal, it could be sold in Fargo for less than half the price.

As usual, William wasted no time in exploiting the discovery. With two partners he formed the Washburn Land Company and purchased almost 114,000 empty acres at $1.00 per acre 20 miles north of Bismarck. In May 1899, with his new general manager, Walter Macomber, who had been with him in Anoka operations since 1873, William located the site for the town named Wilton. By July 1900, two months after the presence of substantial coal deposits had been confirmed, they completed construction of the railroad to the town. This, of course, meant another triumphal celebration with another trainload of dignitaries. Because the coal was only 50 feet down, by September 1900 there were already two crews mining as well as working on a shaft. In two weeks time they were bringing out 50 tons a day, not enough to meet the demand. Two coal chutes and a large boarding house sprung up almost overnight.

William always liked the best. He brought in a generating plant from Bismarck, so he could have electrically-powered machinery in the mine as well as lights in Wilton. In October, he purchased 30,000 feet of lumber for construction. By the end of the year, he had over a thousand feet of electrically-lighted tunnel completed and his production had increased to 200 tons a day. Electrically powered cables hauled empty coal cars in and full ones out. For the workers, he built company bath houses, supplied Thanksgiving turkeys, and a Christmas holiday dinner for employees and families. He established medical facilities and had local doctors on call until finding a full-time doctor.

William began building houses near the boarding house. They eventually formed a settlement with 30 buildings, which he named Chapin, after a favorite Universalist minister (whose name he had already given as a middle name to his son Edwin). Railroad sidings were built near the mine tipple for loading railroad cars, where there were also company offices and a home for the mine manager. Electric-powered fans provided ventilation through two airshafts. During December 1901, the work force doubled from one hundred to two hundred men.

Demand for William's coal was high, and during that first winter the mine operated 20 hours a day, seven days a week, to keep up with it. The lignite fetched $2.10 per ton in Bismarck and $4.00 per ton in St. Paul. William, always good at public relations, never lost an opportunity to bring in the local press—in his private car, of course—to tout the benefits of his

State Historical Society of North Dakota

Washburn's North Dakota steamboat *Expansion*, loafing on the Upper Missouri River on a hot summer day.

product for heating homes. "There is little smoke and soot, fire can be built as readily as wood, and it burns without a clinker," wrote one North Dakota reporter.[82] In a much publicized test in March 1902, a lignite-powered locomotive supposedly pulled 43 loaded freight cars for 105 miles with a savings of more than 40 percent in fuel costs. Lignite was even used on the wood-burning steamer *Expansion*, driving it for 75 miles up the Missouri River at one tenth the cost of wood. (There was no word on the alterations that must have been made to the engines—either before or after the experiment.)

By the time William incorporated the Washburn Lignite Coal Company in December 1902, the mine's output was 475 tons a day. It would rise to 1,000 tons a day that winter. While many miners left to help on nearby farms during harvest time, the mine had plenty of workers—Ukrainians, Swedes, Germans, and Norwegians, as well as "Yankees"—during the high-demand winter months. By 1907 there was a second settlement of company houses, which William named Langhorn (after his youngest son Stanley's new wife). Both his sons Edwin and Stanley were pulled to help manage the mine. Stanley's turn came during the 1920's, when lessened demand for lignite led to cutbacks and a period of intense

---

82   *Wilton News*, September, 1902.

The pagoda-influenced depot in
Wilton, North Dakota, 1971.

labor troubles.[83] (His son Langhorne remembered the harsh winters and fights at school.)

By 1910, eight hundred people lived near Wilton. Five years later, Washburn Lignite Coal Company employed four hundred men and produced 1,500 tons of coal every day, said to make it the largest lignite mine in the world.[84]

While most country railroad stations were made from standard company plans, Wilton had a special depot. William needed a place to stay during his visits. The bones of the Wilton station were the same as the others on the Soo Line, but the family's visit to China and its pagodas had lingered in their memories. Wilton got a pagoda-influenced station— perhaps the only pagoda imitation in North Dakota— and William got his upstairs apartment in a building that still stands.

William now had a castle, three titles, and a prairie empire that included a third railroad. But he was also 73 years old. Perhaps not surprisingly he was happy to sell the railroad to his former colleagues at the Soo Line in 1904.

The buyers had reservations about the seller. Straight-talking Fred Underwood, now vice president of the Soo, and Edward Pennington, his general manager, exchanged revealing letters after the deal was completed, with Pennington writing, "This is the third railroad that the Senator has built and sold out; I hope the last one. He was very fortunate in being able to unload this one." Underwood answered, "I hope, with you, that the Senator is now out of the transportation business. I think he realizes that he ought to be out of it."[85]

---

83   There is no record of significant labor troubles during William's lifetime at any of his enterprises. He paid well, and conditions were good.

84   Frances Wold, "Washburn Lignite Coal Company, A History of Mining at Wilton, North Dakota," in *North Dakota History Magazine*, 43 (Fall 1976): 12.

85   Pennington to Underwood, May 12, 1904, and Underwood to Pennington, May 16, 1904, Soo Line collection, J. J. Hill Reference Library, St. Paul.

People who knew Washburn slightly thought him formal and cold, and many business colleagues did not like him—perhaps because of William's impatience with the details of managing. To political colleagues and those who knew him well, however, he seemed more personable. After William's death, his friend George Brackett admitted William's "naturally aristocratic" bearing but noted that when people knew him better, he was "affable, approachable, amiable, and in every way a charming man." Yet, Brackett continued, "Washburn had a manner about him that was not the kind of manner to make a man popular with men. It was just his natural dignity."[86] Brackett, five years younger and with less formal education than Washburn, may have been awed by William. Brackett had also had been in Alaska during most of William's time on the Pillsbury-Washburn management committee.

If Brackett could have seen the desperate poverty of the Washburn farm in Livermore during the decade before William's birth, he may not have considered Washburn a well-born aristocrat. In fact, the Washburn family cupboard in Maine was so bare that brother Elihu was shipped to grandparents in Massachusetts to leave more food for younger siblings. The family also had the disgrace of bankruptcy and a sheriff's sale of their possessions. Although William was born after these events took place, he apparently never shared the story with his friends or associates.

At any rate, William's patrician public image was about to take a terrible change for the worse. Like a great storm cloud rising to obscure the prairies, a towering financial catastrophe would end his long—very long—string of extraordinary successes and triumphs. The whirlwind would obscure everything he had done before it came and erase his name from the history of the city he had worked so long to create. Going to its knees with him would be the largest flour company in the world.

---

86   Gaillard Hunt, "The Life of William Drew Washburn," 9–10, manuscript, Washburn Family Papers.

9

Icarus Melts
1908–1910

The normally calm boardroom was in a most un-British uproar. The walls and windows of the staid sanctum in London's banking district shook with enraged voices. Some of the most respected financial men in London leaped to their feet, faces livid and fists shaking in the air or pounding the long table. Gone was their veneer of Victorian manners, their habit of understatement. Americans—a gang of country bumpkins out on the prairies— had snookered them, and they were frustrated, angry, and deeply embarrassed. Britannia might rule the waves, but they had been mislead, lied to, and—worst of all— robbed. Somebody was going to have to pay.

William Washburn's finale, like his whole life, was almost mythical in proportion. In fact, ancient Greek mythology includes the tale of Icarus and his father Daedalus, who were imprisoned on Crete by a wicked king. Daedalus fashioned a pair of wings from wax and feathers to enable his son to escape. He warned him not to fly too close to the sun, but Icarus was overcome by the joy of his flight and forgot the advice. As he soared higher and higher, the hot sun melted the wax of his wings, and Icarus fell to his death in the sea.

William Drew Washburn was a modern Icarus. He swooped through dozens of enterprises, but none of his flights matched his career in the flour milling business. By the time of Cadwallader Washburn's death in 1882, William owned two large flour mills: the Palisade Mill in Minneapolis and the Lincoln Mill in Anoka. In addition, he controlled the company supplying waterpower to mills on the west side of the Falls of St. Anthony. His audacious move in 1889 to join his businesses with Pillsbury milling interests on the east bank and then to sell the whole works to the British—

all the while retaining management control in local hands—represented a spectacular coup. Washburn and the Pillsburys prospered significantly from the new Pillsbury-Washburn Flour Mills Company, Ltd.

William's reputation in Minneapolis did not seem to suffer much from the maneuver. Support for him as a U.S. senator was stronger in the city than elsewhere in the state. The troubling fact that the city's biggest business was now in the hands of investors thousands of miles away was offset by the mills still being run by local people and still providing an expanding number of jobs. Local good will was strengthened by the clear intention of the new owners to expand the business right where it was.

Following the buy-out, British investors generously poured in funds to improve the acquisition. They anticipated a good return on their investment— annual profits of $900,000 a year and a 15 percent dividend on ordinary shares,

Minnesota Historical Society

Engineer William De la Barre took maximum advantage of every technological advance to enhance the production of water power at the falls, making the power-generation side of Pillsbury-Washburn its most dependable profit center.

according to the new company's prospectus. Mills were enlarged, new machinery installed, and new elevators built. Production steadily increased. The company introduced products such as breakfast cereals and built a new mill exclusively designed to produce them. Regional sales offices opened, and a force of salaried salesmen was created.[87]

Across the river, the Washburn-Crosby milling company was also doing well. The fact that the two largest milling operations in town each

---

87 The Pillsbury C Mill, as well as the introduction of early oatmeal products, is described in William Powell, *Pillsbury's Best, A Company History from 1869* (Minneapolis: Pillsbury Company, 1985), 55–57.

Hennepin County Library

Pillsbury-Washburn's new company headquarters occupied several floors of Minneapolis's fourteen-story Guarantee Loan building, said to be the first skyscraper west of Chicago.

carried the name of a different Washburn brother in their titles apparently had little effect on sales.

Milling returns for Pillsbury-Washburn could vary from year to year, but the cash cow for the company was its waterpower operation, which the British moved aggressively to make more efficient. East-side and west-side waterpower companies were combined into a single management, and William De la Barre, a respected engineer, was put in charge of both.

To take advantage of the new technology of long-distance power transmission, a second dam was built slightly downstream of the original dams and a new power station added. The Twin City Rapid Transit Company, under the direction of William's old Soo Line railroad partner Thomas Lowry, began to convert from horse-drawn to electrically-powered street cars. In 1897, Lowry signed a 40-year lease for power from the new dam.

Company headquarters was moved into a 14-story skyscraper—said to be the first built west of Chicago.[88] Pillsbury-Washburn soon eclipsed all other producers in town. In 1899, 10 years after the buy-out, the company's annual production hit an astounding 5.3 million barrels. It was the largest flour miller in the world.

But appearances were deceptive.

As in any commodity-based business, the biggest expense for millers each year was the price paid for wheat. The bigger their annual production,

---

88   This was the Guarantee Loan Building, later called the Metropolitan Life Building.

the more wheat they needed. Although the millers steadily improved efficiency and reinvested profits into new facilities, their biggest expense by far remained the wheat itself. As early as 1866, George Brackett and 130 area flour millers had joined together to form the cooperative Minnesota Millers Association to buy wheat. But in trying to insure adequate supplies, there were factors they could not control. The production of wheat—as every farmer well knew—was subject to a host of variables.

Foremost was rainfall—there had to be enough to germinate the planted seed, but not too much to turn the field into a bog or sweep away the new plants. Rain couldn't be too violent, either. Summer hailstorms or tornadoes, common across the plains, could ruin an entire crop in just a few minutes. When the rains stopped, or were late, or didn't come at all, sun-baked fields were often subject to dust storms and insects. Huge clouds of locusts could decimate a crop for miles in every direction. Timing—when to plant and when to harvest—was also important.

Throughout the growing season each year, these variables resulted in many different grades of wheat kernels. The heavier the kernels, the more millers would pay farmers for them and the better chance farmers would have to clear a profit. Farmers had expenses to recoup, from the cost of land and seed to the cost of labor or labor-saving machinery. How far did they have to haul their products to the nearest elevators? What were buyers paying there, and what freight rate was the railroad charging? Would farmers be able to recoup the costs of the seed planted months earlier?

The price millers paid to farmers varied inversely to the amount of wheat farmers had to sell. If the supply of wheat got ahead of the demand for flour, then the price for wheat began to drop. The more wheat there was, the lower the price got. So when wheat production across the prairies boomed during the 1890s, the price of wheat fell.

On the surface this might seem a boon for millers. But millers took orders for flour and signed contracts to buy wheat long before the wheat was actually harvested. As millers vastly expanded their capacity to purchase and hold wheat until it was needed, the landscape across the plains was not only laced with rail lines. It was also studded with grain elevators. Near the mills themselves huge new terminal elevators rose up into the sky.

In this way millers insured themselves inventory to cover increasing orders. Even if the crop was poor, they would have surplus from the previous year to carry them through. At Pillsbury-Washburn, the policy was to carry two million bushels of wheat—about a two-month supply.[89] But if the year's crop was good and prices fell, this could mean that the expense of the wheat in the miller's bins far exceeded its market value by the time they milled it. The difference became critical at the end of the company's fiscal year.

The magic date for Pillsbury-Washburn each year was August 31, when the company's entire inventory of wheat had to be valued not on the basis of what the company had paid for it, but on the price of wheat on the open market that day. In 1892, for example, the company paid 96 cents a bushel for an enormous inventory with a market value of only 78 cents on August 31. This meant an unexpected charge against earnings of $418,841. It happened again in 1893 and 1894—with charges of almost $800,000 and more than $500,000, respectively. As a result, several hundred British investors who were expecting a return of as much as 12 percent on their preferred shares in the company were greatly disappointed.

Millers could protect themselves from price fluctuations to some degree by a process called "hedging." When millers ordered wheat, they could also purchase a futures contract to sell an equal amount of wheat at the same price. The contract would come due on the same date they expected to grind the first lot. When that date arrived, any gain or loss in the price of wheat was immediately offset by an opposite gain or loss in the futures contract. Thus the mill was protected from fluctuation in the price of wheat between purchase and milling time.

But futures contracts cost money, and as Pillsbury-Washburn's needs increased and profit-margins narrowed, futures contracts began to appeal less to cost-conscious managers. The company's buyers roamed wheat country and were in a good position to predict the size and quality of the coming crop. The company assumed its predictions were as good as anybody else's. So, eventually, the company no longer hedged much of its inventory with futures contracts. This meant losses every time the grain crop was good and the price of grain went down.

---

89   Powell, *Pillsbury's Best*, 53.

The whaleback grain carrier S. S. *Washburn* was launched in 1892.

In 1893, as Pillsbury-Washburn tried to cut back on the size of its wheat inventory, a bank panic hit that resulted in a national economic depression for the next five years. Orders slowed, and the average price the company could get for their flour declined from $4.12 a barrel in 1892 to $2.83 in 1896. The company was forced to reduce wages of its employees for most of 1895. The numbers got better in 1895 and 1896, when the company correctly anticipated a wheat shortage and increased their buying to take advantage of the consequent rise in wheat prices. In addition they introduced a broad policy of hedging on all purchases, despite its dampening effect on profits.

On November 12, 1897, a weary Charles A. Pillsbury turned the management of the company over to Henry L. Little, with the blessing of the company's British owners. Little, first hired by Charles as an office boy in 1879, had steadily risen within the company. Calling him "an honorable, conscientious, right-thinking and straight-running man, with great ability and much courage and energy"[90], the *Northwestern Miller* hailed Little's appointment.

---

90 *Northwestern Miller*, November. 19, 1897, p. 815.

Little earned his stripes in 1898, when he successfully helped fend off Thomas A. McIntyre's attempt to make Pillsbury-Washburn part of an enormous trust of 15 large mills stretching from New York to Minnesota. Many British investors wished to sell out, but the Americans bought enough shares to insure that McIntyre's scheme failed. Little did a masterful job of securing the support of key customers.

For the nine years between 1890 and 1899, Pillsbury-Washburn's average profit on every bushel of wheat it milled was less than a cent-and-a-half. Charles Pillsbury once told a reporter that even the closest and most calculating farmer in the state said that the profit ought to have been three cents a bushel.[91] (At Pillsbury's death in 1899, William Washburn was among the honorary pallbearers.)

Throughout these difficult years, William seemed impervious to reversals. His opinions were sought by local newspapers wherever he went. He represented solid respectability in a world that was less than 60 years removed from being a frontier—a world that eagerly embraced the images of permanence and success that he delighted in projecting. He had had many titles. At various times he had been called agent, partner, trustee, general, president, congressman, senator, chairman—even doctor. But his stints as a manager had all been short and unhappy. When he succeeded to the chairmanship of the American management committee of Pillsbury-Washburn, once again the experience would not end happily.

William was probably not involved in any day-to-day decisions at Pillsbury-Washburn. The company continued to limit its inventories of wheat and successfully survived a lengthy strike of its workers in 1903. However, with the exception of 1904, the company's performance never came close to British owners' expectations. Company management blamed poor-quality wheat, expensive wheat, declines in prices that could be charged for products, declines in foreign trade, and excessive competition.

From 1901 through 1904, the U.S. wheat crop declined by a quarter while demand continued to increase. Between 1904 and 1908, the crop increased slightly but still totaled less than eight years earlier. In 1908,

91   Powell, *Pillsbury's Best*, 65.

although the company's five mills reported average production totaling an amazing 31,800 barrels of flour per day, the high price of raw wheat to sustain this huge production meant that the millers' profits continued to stagnate. That year the *Wall Street Journal* reported that, excluding profits from the waterpower company, Pillsbury-Washburn's net profits were less than 2 percent of net sales.[92]

It had been a trying few years for the company. William made a splash in 1905 by leading a move among American shareholders to move the company's domicile to the United States to avoid English inheritance taxes, but the proposal never reached a vote. In May 1905 Henry Little reportedly made heavy purchases of May wheat in an attempt to corner the market. Despite Little's reputation for skillful purchasing, the 1907 earnings were again disappointing. Ominously, the directors announced that grain prices, in the wake of springtime crop damage, had been forced up 30 or 40 percent by grain speculators, making profitable milling impossible for several months.

Weather-related fluctuations in the wheat prices could be turned into wild gyrations by speculators—gamblers who traded for the sole purpose of fast profits from the trade itself. Rumors of crop failures, for example, could bring in a flood of orders for grain futures from anyone who thought they knew differently. Sudden purchasing or selling could greatly exaggerate swings in prices whatever the actual supply. If a gambler guessed wrong, the futures contract price still had to be paid on the contract-specified date. If borrowed money was involved, the circumstances became stickier.

For some time, rumors had circulated that Pillsbury-Washburn managers' speculations had affected both profits and losses. Although vehemently denied by London board chairman Richard H. Glyn, and unsubstantiated by anything in the company's books, rumors continued to circulate.

Then, on May 16, 1908, the company told its British investors that payment of a preference dividend would have to be indefinitely postponed. The real bombshell came in a letter from the board to shareholders on August 12. To the astonishment and consternation of the

92 *Wall Street Journal*, August 26, 1908.

investment world, the largest flour miller in the world announced that it had gone into receivership. All the assets of Pillsbury-Washburn were suddenly put into the hands of the courts.[93]

Alfred Pillsbury, the 38-year-old son of John S. Pillsbury, together with his twin cousins, Charles S. and John S. (sons of Charles A. Pillsbury), had first learned about the company's trouble when called in by the company's three principal bankers. The trio was led by Clive T. Jaffray, a vice president of the First National Bank of Minneapolis. Jaffray had just been playing golf with a prominent grain dealer who told him that Pillsbury-Washburn was in trouble because of unauthorized speculations by its president. William Washburn—76 years old, recently retired chairman of the management committee, and absent from Minneapolis much of the year—probably received the news at about the same time.

When the three young Pillsburys scrambled back to their offices, they learned that not only was the company almost out of cash, but that it owed approximately one million dollars on notes issued in the company's name but not recorded in its books. The liability was far in excess of anything either the Pillsburys or their bankers cared to loan to the company.

All efforts to obtain further credit in Europe and the United States were unsuccessful. With an average of $900,000 in notes coming due each month from August through December, the company's only choices were declaring bankruptcy or continuing operations under a receiver. As strongly urged by creditors and the Pillsburys, the American management committee hastily chose the latter. In London, the stunned board voted not to oppose the proceedings.

In response to the complaint by five banks and John S. Pillsbury, Judge Myron Purdy ordered receivership on August 8 and immediately appointed three receivers: Albert C. Loring, much-respected head of Consolidated Milling Company, Charles S. Pillsbury, and Albert C. Cobb, a prominent attorney representing the banks.

In Minneapolis, at first there was fear that the city's largest employer was about to shut its doors. Then there was anger that malfeasance on

---

93   This story was well covered by the *Minneapolis Journal* (August 8–13, December 1, 12, 1908, and June 23, 1909) and by the *Northwestern Miller* (August 1908–July 1910). The best overall report, however, was published 75 years later in Powell, *Pillsbury's Best*, 73–93.

such a scale could have been going on without the company or its auditors knowing it. In London, investors were totally surprised, and then furious. They loudly demanded retribution.

The first step to be taken was a full audit of company assets. When this was completed, it became clear that the healthiest part of the company was its waterpower-generation business run under the watchful eye of William De la Barre. Not far behind was the storage-elevator business —over a hundred elevators generating steady profits under the management of Charles Amsden. The milling business was found to be structurally sound, its equipment in good repair, its operations efficient, and its customers solvent. However— incredibly—the company had outstanding financial obligations of more than five million dollars and nowhere near enough money in the till to pay them.

The committee of creditors that was formed consisted entirely of Minneapolis banks—representing what was estimated to be as many as two hundred banks holding Pillsbury-Washburn outstanding paper.[94] Although the company's obligations had been caused by speculation in wheat futures, it was the banks that had financed the unauthorized trading, making loans on collateral pledged but never seen. Over the years, these banks had grown large on the proceeds of loans to the millers. Now these same banks were scrambling to avoid going over the cliff with their biggest customer.

No criminal charges were ever filed despite a renegade group of British shareholders' hard fight. They pointed to previously hidden ledgers that contained unaccounted-for transactions. They claimed they had been given fraudulent reports and that the company's auditors and top managers should have known what was happening. Minneapolis banks had been kept equally in the dark while they continued to extend their lines of credit, and they were as unaware as their British cousins even though they operated within a few city blocks of the unknown and unauthorized trading.

Ironically, since the company's business was fundamentally sound and its customers still wanted four, orders from major customers all over the

---

94 *Wall Street Journal*, August 11, 1908.

world kept pouring in. If something could be worked out in the courts, the banks stood a good chance of getting their loans repaid.

And so, on both sides of the Atlantic, the scrambling to save the company began. As the city lay suspended between gloom and optimism, power brokers negotiated—with the court looking on. Opposing camps fell into roughly three groups. In Minneapolis were the American managers and shareholders, including the Pillsbury family that had both the means and the motivation to save the situation. Also in Minneapolis were the financiers—the creditors on whose largesse the company's future operations depended but from whom no mercy could be expected unless loans could be repaid. Finally, in London, there were outraged British shareholders, with little knowledge of the milling business, not enough resources to save the company, and likely to take the highest losses or wait the longest for any payback.

The most grievous sin appeared to be the "hidden ledger." It contained unrecorded notes carrying the signatures of three officers of the company: Henry L. Little, president, L. P. Hubbard, treasurer, and Charles Amsden, manager of the elevator operation. President Little, while denying that speculation had led to the company's downfall, resigned on August 10 and left the city, leaving word that he would be travelling indefinitely. Hubbard, who had been with the company for 35 years, retired a week later. Amsden stayed on, said nothing, and eventually resigned. The rest of the management committee, including ex-chairman Washburn, was left to contemplate their sins—of either commission or omission.

Looking back it is difficult to see William as personally guilty of the fraud that so angered the London shareholders and directors. Personal integrity was a family hallmark, and rectitude characterized his personal life. In addition, he had consistently opposed speculation in any commodity. But Washburn was known to be careless and impatient with the details of managing his enterprises. He got things started, but then did best when he turned details over to others. He had been a good figurehead for the company—distinguished in appearance and manner, with a long record of public service. He had great success in promoting, persuading investors, and presenting his dreams in ways that impressed and inspired.

It is easy to visualize him persuading bankers to lend with only the sketchiest idea of an operation's financial health.

Unlike Charles A. Pillsbury, who enjoyed gambling with grain purchases and the excitement and uncertainty of the market, William would have left the actual figuring to others. His sin was the sin of not paying attention. He saw his post as an honorary one—a disengaged elder statesman.

Outsiders believed the company's problems stemmed from Pillsbury-Washburn's corporate culture. Charles A. Pillsbury had been a high roller who had lost heavily during previous speculations. Henry Little claimed that he had just been trying to make money to cover up these losses, but William H. Dunwoody, one of a series of excellent managers behind the success at Washburn-Crosby across the river, thought this a poor excuse: "I think the whole of their organization was demoralized by the speculative disposition of their predecessor," he observed.[95]

In September 1908, accountants completed their report and listed Pillsbury-Washburn's liquid assets as only a little over two million dollars and its general liabilities as more than five million dollars. Of this amount, $1,758,000 of indebtedness was duly noted in a secret ledger but never reported in the company's financial statements. Furthermore, accountants concluded, irregularities appeared to have commenced about May 1905, a time when Henry Little was reported to have attempted to corner the May wheat market in Minneapolis. William was still chairing the American committee responsible for overseeing the management of the company at this time.

With creditors threatening to shut down the company at any minute, negotiators in England at last hammered out a plan of reorganization. A new operating company would be formed—primarily with Pillsbury money—to purchase Pillsbury-Washburn's liquid assets, to repay creditors with cash and mortgage bonds, and to lease the mills and other properties. The plan was presented to shareholders for approval on November 26, but due to fiery calls for restitution and criminal prosecution of unnamed miscreants, the meeting was adjourned for five days. Cooler heads finally prevailed. The plan was

95   Powell, *Pillsbury's Best*, 80.

then approved on December 1, but contention continued and negotiations almost broke down twice. After their representative conferred in the United States with the company's American creditors and shareholders, final approval by British shareholders was at last achieved on June 7, 1909. That same month, the new company incorporated in Minneapolis as the Pillsbury Flour Mills Company. Most of the two million dollars in capital for the new company was provided by three Pillsburys and their friends. The name of Washburn was conspicuously absent from the new organization.

Opposition to the deal had not disappeared, however. British board members, disgruntled over receivership expenses, held up discharging the receivers until after the annual shareholders meeting in July 1910. Two directors, Frank Spencer and George Cloutte, both of whom had been to Minneapolis to obtain first-hand particulars, openly broke with the rest of the board. Cloutte sent a letter to shareholders with his own account of the "frauds in question," which included banks honoring checks with only one signature and one bank not giving auditors information about a hidden account. Although newspapers in Minneapolis were discreet, scandal sheets in New York had a field day. "Pillsbury Men Who Got Millions to Be Prosecuted" shouted one tabloid.[96]

The July meeting was tempestuous. The London reporter for the *Northwestern Miller* reported hearing the words "swindled," "robbed," "cheated," and "fleeced." Cloutte rose to call the situation "one of the greatest company scandals of modern times" and accused the directors of allowing Henry L. Little to "become a sort of general dictator" and "not exercising the vigilance . . . they ought to have exercised." Stockholder threats to sue for restitution were reported in London, Chicago, and Minneapolis.[97] Young John S. Pillsbury and Ralph Whelan, the family lawyer, were on hand to take the heat. They patiently explained the unhappy choices: either accept their offer and hope for some return in the future, or kill the company and lose everything now. At last, the new company was accepted, and a new board was appointed.

---

96 *New York Press*, July 10, 1910.

97 Variously reported in the *Chicago Daily Tribune* and *Minneapolis Journal*, July 22, 1910.

Efforts seeking restitution continued despite American moves to bury them. It took 18 months and almost 50 legal documents before Little gave up some mining stock and Amsden surrendered his company stock. Pillsbury-Washburn turned over all its grain elevator assets to the new company, and both companies gave up any further claims or rights. No criminal proceedings or restitution suits were pursued publicly.

Minneapolis was not only a relatively new town, but it was similar to a small town in that its business elite was also its political elite. Relatively few people seemed to run everything. They knew and trusted each other, and a threat to one was a threat to all—especially if that threat came from outside the town. Bad news had to be absorbed quietly so that business could continue. This was the spirit in which labor unrest had been quashed in 1904 and previous economic crises had been weathered.

The fall of Pillsbury-Washburn Company was one of the greatest shocks the city had sustained. When the Pillsburys stepped in to save the company, the action also seemed to save the city from foreigners and promised to return the mills to local control. While the former managers were quickly and quietly removed from the scene, the new generation of Pillsburys used their own fortunes to smooth over the troubled waters and return the company to its former health. Even the *Northwestern Miller*, although it muttered about the company being "undermined by wrong methods, and mismanagement, coupled with misuse of a magnificent credit," advised British investors that they were better off after the family bought the company.[98] The flour market was strong, and good times would return.

But a nagging, and fundamental, question remained. Who had brought foreigners into the company to begin with? Who had put quick profit ahead of local owners who really knew the business? Who but the chairman of the American management committee should have been watching the store? Charles A. Pillsbury was dead, and his sons were pledging their family's honor and fortunes to put the situation right.

But there sat William Drew Washburn, supposedly preening himself at Fair Oaks while the catastrophe happened all around him. True, he was

---

98 *Northwestern Miller*, September 16, 1908, p. 705, and October 21, 1908, p. 171.1910.

not the only member of the American management committee. Beside the departed Little and Amsden, William De la Barre and young Alfred Pillsbury had sat on that committee. But William was the chairman, and he clearly had the responsibility to oversee the managers and the power to overrule them, if necessary.

We can never know William's exact involvement, let alone his liability. William De la Barre, who was probably lucky to avoid being a target himself, wrote in 1910 about responsibility to outraged London board member Frank Spencer: "H. L. L[ittle] is in another state. W. D. W[ashburn] has one foot in the grave and has no guilt. A. F. P[illsbury] has his wealth tied up in the leasing company, and has no guilt. C. M. A[msden] will make a strong fight. L. P. H[ubbard] is on the Pacific coast [and] has no money. Who is next? I don't know. Do you?"[99]

Undoubtedly the British were misled—mostly by their own enthusiasms, but probably also by overly optimistic projections by company managers. Bankers in Minneapolis were also misled. They extended themselves, as they had always done, to provide financing to their biggest customer. They must have been offered collateral to back up these loans. Of course, the history of banking is full of tales of nonexistent collateral. Bankers can accuse customers of lying, but bankers also have responsibility to be diligent and make sure exposure is covered by hard assets.

William may have been careless, but he was not intentionally dishonest. Like Icarus, the joy of the flight overcame prudence, and he never noticed that his wings were melting.

True to their pledges in the reorganization agreements, the British shareholders with the heaviest losses did not initiate criminal action, but they had other ways—much quieter ways—to seek restitution. Their New York lawyers investigated, drew conclusions, and quietly took action.

Over the next two years, William Drew Washburn's assets and income began to wane. The first sign appeared in an announcement by the city of Minneapolis in 1910 that William, in an act of unprecedented "generosity," had made a great gift to the city. He offered his entire Fair Oaks property—the castle, greenhouse, gardens, stables, ponds and grounds— for future use as an art museum. He requested only that he and

---

99   Powell, *Pillsbury's Best*, 93.

Hennepin County Library

In this last known photograph of William Washburn, he is still immaculately turned out.

his wife be allowed to live their last days there, a request which city fathers happily granted. Presumably, this also relieved William of having to pay property taxes on the expensive estate.

William himself never made any public comment. His name disappeared from the press and he stayed away from Minneapolis. Lengthy summer gatherings at Livermore and sojourns to take the waters at Carlsbad filled his time. When he became seriously ill there two years later, he sailed home from Europe, was met with a private rail car loaned by former associates, emerged in Minneapolis frail but still impeccably turned out, and took his last carriage ride home. A few days later, on July 24, 1912, William died at Fair Oaks. His race through life had lasted more than 81 very full years.

With William gone, life at Fair Oaks for Lizzy must have been quiet and lonely. After a respectable interval, she joined her son Edwin in New Jersey, where she died in 1916.

Various Minneapolis charities occupied Fair Oaks, but it was expensive to maintain and heat the cavernous building. In 1924, the city paid demolition crews $90,000 to tear it down. Today, only park land remains to mark the spot. The Minneapolis Institute of Arts that faces the space is located on adjacent land given by William's cousin Clinton Morrison.

What happened to William's assets upon his death? He may well have sold them and spent the money to keep up his lifestyle. But even so, the news from the Hennepin County Probate Court which settled his estate in 1912 was remarkable—not for the assets that were there, but for the assets that were not.

There were no further bequests in William's will to match his gift of Fair Oaks to the city. Indeed, there were few assets left. His total estate was evaluated at $104,000. Gone were thousands of acres of timberlands, real estate in Anoka and Minneapolis, and farms in Minnesota and North Dakota. Gone were the stock and bonds from his many enterprises—no flour mills, no power company, no railroads, no coal mines, no streetcar companies, no electric light companies, no newspapers, no iron foundry, no harvester works. His estate, in fact, showed every sign of having been quietly but thoroughly cleaned out.

Icarus had crashed. His flight had reached from a rocky ridge in western Maine to the court of the Emperor of China. He had built enterprises ranging from sawmills and coal mines to steamboats and streetcars, acquired forests, dammed rivers, built and rebuilt factories, and helped make a city. He had thrust a thousand miles of railroad across an empty landscape and helped fill up three states with new citizens. He had known power from the halls of Congress to the heart of London and wealth that dazzled a generation.

His flight had ended. Barely a ripple remained to mark his passage— beyond his offspring, who would be quite remarkable in their own right.

10

Afterwards
1910–1965

The Pillsbury-Washburn Company's fall from grace was swift, but its death was slow.

In 1914 the *London Times* reported: "The [company] meeting Thursday next might just as well not be held. Except the few arithmetical details . . . there is nothing whatever to communicate. . . . Since the company's reorganization in 1909, following on a receivership and some very unsavory disclosures, the shareholders might just as well have been nonexistent for any benefit they have received. . . . There is not a flicker of hope for the Ordinary shareholders."[100]

In 1929, historian Charles Kuhlman pronounced the company's epitaph: "The new company soon put the properties on a paying basis. The old company was unable to pay dividends on its heavy capitalization, and, when, in 1923, they were faced with the alternative of buying out the operating company or selling to it, they were forced to sell. . . . There seems to be no question that the native Minneapolis interests—and especially the Pillsbury family—are once more dominant in it."[101]

William's infrequent presence in Minneapolis, judging by the paucity of local newspaper coverage, may have suited city leaders eager to put the Pillsbury-Washburn affair behind them. In July 1912 William was buried in a family plot at Minneapolis's Lakewood Cemetery, which he had helped establish. His small stone was one among several fronting a modest obelisk reading "Washburn," not unlike similar markers around it for other prominent families of the city.

---

100 *London Times*, January 5, 1914, p. 15.

101 Charles Byron Kuhlman, *The Development of the Flour-Milling Industry in the United States* (Boston: Houghton Mifflin Co., 1929), 172.

Although William had time in his last years to tell his story—as his brothers Elihu and Charles told theirs—and although three of his sons were published writers and journalists, none of them took on the job. On the contrary, the rumor around Livermore was that William, Jr., slowly destroyed every written record of his father's life. For example, William Washburn's siblings took great pleasure in keeping a family journal at Livermore. Samuel made nautical observations of every day's weather and records of crops planted and harvested. Israel, Jr., began his political commentary and reminiscences with Maine's statehood in 1820. Charles filled pages with moody self-reflections, and both Cadwallader and Elihu left voluminous reports and recordings of family comings and goings. Seven colorful volumes cover a period of 60 years. All the brothers are there—except for Young Rapid, who probably spent more time in Livermore during his last years than all his siblings combined.

(A small collection of correspondance between William and his brother Sidney does survive in the Duke University Library in Durham. It consists mostly of hastily written notes about money. Sid made literally hundreds of short-term loans to William—enough so that, in the last years of his life, Sid realized a comfortable living from the interest received from these notes.)

Records elsewhere are similarly bare. Following newspaper coverage of William's final race home to die, encomiums were generous but short-lived. Some testimony seemed a bit forced. James Stroud Bell, president of Washburn-Crosby, called William "a grand old man in every sense of the word" and "a prominent figure in the development of the great resources of the northwest country."[102] These were kind words from the gentle man who had fired William from Washburn-Crosby in 1889. Whereas the Wisconsin Historical Society published a book of memorials shortly after brother Cadwallader died, it was three years before the Minnesota Historical Society gave William a single-page tribute.

Oddly, William may have left a bigger lasting impression in Livermore than he did in Minneapolis. He improved the mansion, and many of the furnishings there today came from Fair Oaks—most notably large oil portraits of William and Lizzie. William also acquired adjoining properties that added tracts of meadow and forest until the original 65 acres grew to

---

102 *Minneapolis Journal*, July 30, 1912.

an impressive sweep of 450 acres. William acquired three separate houses to make summer visits easier for his children and built a carriage trail through the woods on nearby Watters Hill to connect the airy summit with the forest pools at the base. Picnic expeditions to the "pools of Simeon" became a favorite summer recreation.

Through all the adventures, all the ups and downs, Lizzie was at William's side to the very end—53 years. Lizzie had always been in the close company of strong men. Her father, Franklin Muzzy, had made himself into one of the most successful entrepreneurs in a town that was full of them. When Lizzie married William, she was intimidated neither by him nor his friends. In her years in Minneapolis, she helped entertain virtually every self-made man in the city, and most of the country's political leaders as well. Some of them, like her stern and solitary brother-in-law C. C. Washburn, were close by for more than 20 years. There is every reason to believe that she relished her adventures with William. Managing life at Fair Oaks, entertaining in Washington and Maine, and traipsing around the world, organizing a party for three hundred or designing a flower bed or meeting the needs of her six children, Lizzie provided a comfortable stage for her larger-than-life husband.

William and Lizzie's six surviving children were, like their father, mostly outspoken, bright, attractive, and in a hurry. They may have been William's most lasting and greatest contribution to the world.

Only the eldest son returned to Minneapolis after finishing college and remained there. Graduating from Yale in 1888, William Drew, Jr., dabbled in agricultural real estate and politics. In 1901 he ran for his father's former legislative seat in 1901 and won. He continued to be reelected for the next 24 years, serving eight terms. He ran unsuccessfully for Congress in 1918, married Florence Savier, had one daughter and three sons, and divorced. He lived his last 16 years as a solitary figure at the Minneapolis Athletic Club, until his death at age 66. He was remembered there for his intellect, constant reading, and the clouds of pipe smoke he trailed behind him.

Cadwallader Lincoln, who lived to be 99, achieved multiple successes. Graduating as valedictorian from Gallaudet College for the deaf in 1890, he won "First Award in Design" at M.I.T. in architecture and then defied his father's wishes by going to Europe to paint. Despite continued threats by his father and lack of financial support, Cad kept to his hard work and his bohemian haunts.

He became a master of the difficult technique of dry point etchings. In the Far East he joined his brother Stanley as a war correspondent for the *Chicago Daily News*, covering the Russo-Japanese War (1904–05) and got many exclusive stories from both sides during the siege of Port Arthur.

Painting and etching in Mexico in 1910 when revolution broke out, he was assigned by the *Daily News* to head the correspondents covering the conflict. Working with note pad in hand in a rented top hat, frock coat, striped pants, spats and white gloves, Cad persuaded Mexican revolutionary leader Francesco Madero to give him an interview. This was the last before Madero's assassination, a huge scoop for the Associated Press. As violence escalated, Cad packed up hundreds of his paintings and etchings and headed for the coast, but when his steamer collided with another vessel and sank, two years of his artwork went to the bottom. He produced nearly a thousand more copper etchings before poor eyesight forced him to give up in favor of painting. His subjects ranged from Polynesian cannibals to his aging father, done not long before William's death. The work is notable for half-smile on William's face and the brilliant red rose in his button hole, a perfect symbol of his father's enigmas and enthusiasms.

Cad developed a colorful system of signing that required its own interpretation, and in 1943, at the age of 77, he got married, mainly so that his bride, Margaret Ohrt, could translate his signs to bewildered audiences. He also conducted experiments with insects, and at age 80 he produced a paper to prove that insects have intelligence. After his death in 1965, Gallaudet College dedicated a new arts center in his name. His artwork hangs in museums around the world.

Cad's younger sister Mary Caroline went east for private school—the venerable Ogontz School outside Philadelphia. After a lavish wedding to journalist Elbert Baldwin at Fair Oaks in 1892, she and her husband moved to Lakewood, New Jersey, where she supported her husband as editor of *Outlook Magazine* and raised five children. She founded the Arden School for Girls in Lakewood, as well as an international summer studies program for college graduate girls in Geneva, Switzerland. Mary dabbled in poetry and wrote a charming memoir of the early years of her mother. During the 1920s she and her husband moved to Europe, where they lived until the outbreak of World War II. She died in New York in 1944.

Sibling Edwin Chapin Washburn, born in 1870, proved to be a better assistant to his father. During construction of the Soo Line, Edwin had many rides in Daniel Willard's locomotive. He too went east to school, Exeter, Lawrenceville, and Yale.[103]

In 1887 Edwin joined the Soo Line, rising from machinist apprentice to salesman. On the side, he wrote four books for teenagers about railroads and early American history.

In 1896 Edwin designed a new railroad coupler and, with his father's backing, established a foundry for manufacturing it. The device was widely accepted. In 1898, his father drafted him to build and manage his new railroad in North Dakota. He started the Wilton coal mine and built grain elevators and boarding houses to house workers. He had the most fun designing and operating one of the two steamboats that the company used on the Missouri River. At the foundry back in Minneapolis he invented and patented more than 50 devices for use by railroads. He married and in 1911 went east to join the Baltimore and Ohio Railroad and rejoin Daniel Willard. It was to his house in Englewood, New Jersey, that Lizzie came after William died. In 1916 Edwin became special assistant to Willard, where he served for the next two decades. Edwin was much loved and admired at the B&O until his death in 1937.

Edwin's younger sister Elizabeth, born in 1874, grew up fully exposed to high politics, high finance, and high society—in Minneapolis, in Washington, and in Europe. She helped her parents entertain lavishly, travelled widely, and even launched a warship. Sent to private schools at home and abroad, she completed her education at Radcliffe College. She was known in Minneapolis for her hostess role at Fair Oaks and for occasional writings. After marrying Hamilton Wright, she went to Kuala Lumpur, where Dr. Wright had a three-year appointment in pathology research on the

---

103 Mentioned by Julia Chase Washburn in *Genealogical Notes of the Washburn Family*, 1895, Washburn Library.

disease beriberi. They had two children there and a third in Baltimore in 1904, where Dr. Wright spent time in research at Johns Hopkins University.

Elizabeth had two more children and published several short stories and a book titled *The Colour of the East* (1914), which was favorably reviewed. The family lived in Washington, D.C., and spent summers in the house at Livermore that her father had built for her. When her husband began research in opium and started to raise awareness about its dangers, Elizabeth joined the cause, and she was active in every international narcotics treaty drawn up after 1913. Elizabeth continued in the antidrug crusade after her husband's death in 1917. In 1924, she was named by President Calvin Coolidge U.S. delegate to the Second Geneva Opium Conference, an appointment that carried full diplomatic powers. She was the first American woman to be so honored. In 1930, she was directly responsible for the passage of the Boggs Act, which introduced mandatory sentencing guidelines for drug violations, and for the establishment of the federal Bureau of Narcotics. When she died in Washington in 1952, Commissioner Anslinger called her "irreplaceable" in the fight against illegal drugs.[104]

Stanley, Elizabeth's younger brother, was charming, impulsive, and an adventurous soul mate for his artist-brother Cadwallader. He went to Hill School and Williams College. Like his sister Elizabeth, he met his future spouse, Alice Langhorne, on the family trip to China in 1898. She was a cousin of the famous Langhorne sisters said to have been inspirations for the Gibson girls.[105] (The couple married in 1906 and were devoted to each other for the next 44 years.)

After leaving Harvard Law School and being a police reporter for the *Minneapolis Journal*, which his father had helped found, Stanley joined the *Chicago Daily News*. With his brother Cadwallader, he reported on the Russo-Japanese War. Chartering a tug boat, they cruised the coast around the besieged city of Port Arthur and as far south as Indochina. Stanley produced exclusive stories and interviews, and Cadwallader added his sketches and paintings. After the war, Stanley wrote his first book, a biography of the Japanese commander General Nogi.

---

104 Obituary, *Washington Evening Star*, February 13, 1952.

105 Illustrator Charles Dana Gibson was married to Alice's cousin Irene Langhorne. Another of the Langhorne sisters married an Englishman and became the famous Lady Astor.

In 1906, at his father's request, Stanley returned to Minneapolis to help his brother Edwin save the family steel business—and to marry Alice Longhorne. In the aftermath of the panic of 1907, saving the company proved futile, and Stanley assisted in the gradual liquidation of the Washburn Steel Company in May 1909. (He noted that 288 creditors were paid in full, and the remaining 10 received got 90 percent of what they were owed.) Ever restless, he returned to exploring and surveying in the Canadian wilderness during the summers of 1909 and 1910, covering the entire thousand miles between Edmonton, Alberta, and Prince Rupert, British Columbia, by pack train and canoe.

Stanley also got involved in politics in Minneapolis. Galvanized by the energetic Theodore Roosevelt, Stanley took great delight in tweaking his father and oldest brother by helping carry Minnesota for the hero of San Juan Hill. Alice even joined the effort when, accompanied by her coach and driver, she knocked on doors and dazzled enough people to carry the senator's old precinct for Roosevelt by 12 votes. William, Sr., taking the waters again at Carlsbad, was indignant. (In 1912 the Republican Party ultimately split and Democrat Woodrow Wilson won the presidency, despite Roosevelt carrying Minnesota over Taft and Wilson combined.)

In 1912, Stanley answered his father's call to North Dakota to help run the family coal company. When war in Europe broke, Stanley took an invitation from *Colliers Weekly* in 1914 to cover it. The *London Times* sent him to Russia, where for 26 months he was the only American reporter covering the Russian front and, later, the communist revolution. Back in the United States, he lectured for the American State Department on behalf of the Russian cause. In 1916, he was with the French army at Verdun and attached to the Romanian Army, and in 1917 he served as a military advisor to the U.S. secretary of state, Robert Lansing. When the United States entered the war, Stanley, a commissioned major in the Officers Reserve Corps, went to Russia again, this time as military aid to the John F. Stevens advisory railroad mission and the Root diplomatic mission. By 1918, Stanley was back in France, where he was wounded, sent home, and promoted to lieutenant colonel. After the war, Stanley did liaison work between the American and Japanese delegations at the 1921 Disarmament Conference.

Stanley and wife with their three children moved to southern New Jersey, settling in Lakewood near his sister Mary. He assembled his memories of war experiences and roughing it in the northwest wilderness into several engaging books. In 1926, he was military aide to Queen Marie of Romania during her U.S. visit. He unsuccessfully ran for Congress in New Jersey as a Republican. Between 1926 and 1928, he commuted to North Dakota as president of the coal company, and he headed the North Dakota Coal Operators Association until 1935. He wrote eight books and a play. Just before his death in 1950, he recalled that as a reporter and soldier he had been with 20 armies in approximately one hundred battles. He was buried at Arlington National Cemetery.

Today, more than a hundred years after his death, the visitor to Minneapolis is challenged to find any sign of William Drew Washburn. He spent more than 50 years furiously building things, yet hardly a one of them can be found today.

Excavations along the Mississippi Riverfront behind the new Mill City Museum—built in the shell of Cadwallader's original A Mill—show traces of the canal that William helped build for his brother and suggest the location of the original dam. But one has to imagine the row of sawmills and scream of saws on that dam, the crash of logs, and the roar of the water. One can only imagine the clattering mills that William brought to that canal, or the high whistles of the steam engines shunting boxcars to the mills over the rickety trestles that William and Cadwallader built. Mill City Museum does house an early freight car, as well as original flour barrels that hint at the process.

Nothing but an empty space marks what William built and rebuilt at Anoka. Abandoned foundations mark the mill sites, and there is no sign of his bank or his opera house. The name Pillsbury-Washburn, once the largest flour operation in the world, is forgotten, along with most memories that the two families ever had a business connection.[106]

---

106 Cadwallader's Company, which became General Mills in 1928, acquired
    Pillsbury in 2001 and now has annual sales of more than $13 billion. It is one
    of *Fortune* magazine's "Most Admired Companies." The fact that there were two
    huge flour mills in direct competition with one another, each with "Washburn"
    in the name, seems to have caused little confusion among the customers who
    bought their products.

William's railroads have all gone through multiple changes of name and ownership, and the "Soo Line" name is rare and faded—where it can be found at all. Washburn Station, on the old Minneapolis and St. Louis line, has been swallowed up by the town of Eden Prairie. His greatest accomplishment, the original Soo Line route, lacks track along some stretches, although grades and right-of-ways still provide trails for snowmobilers and hikers. Where the track is still in use, traffic is intermittent. The yards at Gladstone and Sault Ste. Marie are still busy, though the engines—all diesels—now bear the logo of the Canadian Pacific.

Evidence of the railroad's many years of heavy use are visible to the discerning eye. The bridges are now of sturdy steel and concrete, and the original ballasting, so intermittent in early photographs, has been supplemented so often that the surviving tracks are elevated two feet above their original levels.

No sign remains of the Minneapolis Harvester Works or the Washburn foundry. The North Star Woolen Mill is condominiums. The street railway is now Twin Cities Rapid Transit. The *Minneapolis Journal* is still publishing, through a complicated genealogy, as the *Star Tribune*. In North Dakota, only a few piles of brick and remnants of concrete foundations mark the Washburn Lignite Coal Company, purchased by the Otter Tail Power Company in 1928 and later abandoned.

There is no sign of any of William's three homes in Minneapolis. The mills swallowed up the first, and the second was replaced by commercial enterprises as the city expanded. Of Fair Oaks, only a patch of public park remains. The Minneapolis city hall and court house, dwarfed by skyscrapers, and the library, consolidated with the Hennepin County library system, have little to acknowledge the man who helped start them.

Six landmarks in Minneapolis today carry the Washburn name. The Washburn Center for Children was named for Cadwallader, whose bequest funded it. Washburn Fair Oaks Park and the Washburn Park neighborhood surrounding Washburn High School were named for William, who gave the land. The latter parcel was part of the real estate development William and others started in 1886 along Minnehaha Creek, then on the south edge of the city. It included the land that William offered as a site for the original Washburn Memorial Orphan Asylum. The orphanage building was torn down in 1929, and the present-day Ramsey magnet school marks the site. Today, Washburn High School (completed in 1925) and Washburn Avenue are said to be named after both Cadwallader and William.

William's two main philanthropic interests have fared well, although their names and locations have changed. The Church of the Redeemer became the First Universalist Church of Minneapolis, and its congregation of better than 800 members meets in a handsome former synagogue in the southwestern part of the city. Washburn Center for Children, near the Fair Oaks site, is a busy organization that serves nearly 4,000 families each year.

Ironically, William's traces are more evident in Maine. The family mansion, with its sweeping porch, still crowns the hill in Livermore, and his carriage track has been reclaimed. Two of the three houses he built or bought for his daughters show as only foundations in the woods, but Cadwallader Lincoln's Pond Side cottage is still in use by the Washburn-Norlands Foundation. The roads over which William raced his buggy are paved now, but the winters are no easier than they were when he was growing up there, making them almost as rough as the originals.

With all this impermanence, what significance can we find in William's meteoric career? Most important, he personifies his time. He is every inch an entrepreneur in an age of entrepreneurship. Sometimes his fearlessness seems more like foolishness. As early as 1859, Cadwallader, himself out on a limb at the time, wrote his brother Sidney that William professed "great distress of mind that he has not been able to meet this obligation, all of which I should believe, were he less reckless and extravagant."[107] At the height of William's 1874 financial crisis, as creditors were stripping his assets from him, he responded to an anxious letter from Sidney about the latest overdue loan payment with a light-hearted reply, "Keep cool."[108] From such blitheness sprang mighty deeds, but also tragic defeats.

The frontier was a magnet to restless and impatient souls like William. The horizon stretched forever, and the opportunities were limitless—as were the risks. When new markets appeared, Young Rapid jumped to meet

---

107 Cadwallader C. Washburn to A. Sidney Washburn, October 15, 1859, A. S. Washburn Papers, Duke University Library, Durham, NC.

108 William D. Washburn to A Sidney Washburn, August 4, 1874, A. S. Washburn Papers.

them—lumber to build new towns and cities; flour to feed new arrivals; railroads to supply the new mills and transport their product to new markets; expansions and new technologies to increase production. For pioneer entrepreneurs, anything was possible. Despite severe crises in the economy— William went through three of them between 1857 and 1895—these men and their bankers picked themselves up and tried again.

One of the most constant and calming influences in William's exciting life was surely his deep involvement with the Universalist church. With all his breath-taking plunges in business and top-speed lifestyle came his life-long regular attendance and heartfelt support of its optimistic credo. He once wrote: "We believe that holiness and true happiness are inseparably connected, and that believers ought to be careful to maintain order, and to practice good works for these things are good and profitable unto men. Universalism is the belief that . . . the best possible outcome is to be expected to the human experiment." (William then pointed to the Washburn Orphans Asylum as an example of Universalist benevolence— ironically, since his brother Cadwallader, whose bequest paid for it, was not a known churchgoer.)[109]

While another apparent life contrast can be seen between the idealism of his youth and his later political conservatism, the country changed during his life, and the Republican Party with it. William's stand in favor of state regulation of railroad freight rates reflected his desire to protect businesses from another. Seeing how grain farmers and millers were threatened by railroad rapacity, he decided the proper role for government —whether it was mandated freight rates, or Corps of Engineer improvements to dams and reservoirs, or protective tariffs—was to protect business. This was what the majority of his constituents wanted from their congressman and senator.

So we are left with the image of Icarus, carving glorious circles in the sky, climbing higher and higher, as prudent men below watch in awe and wonder. While the flight lasts, it is indeed spectacular.

---

109 Unidentified paper, probably by William, in Washburn Family Papers.

Appendix

William D. Washburn's Enterprises

Mill companies

Minneapolis Mill Co.	agent, partner	Became Pillsbury-Washburn, Ltd.
C. C. Washburn Co.	partner	WDW removed, reinstated temporarily
Washburn-Crosby Co.	co-manager	WDW removed (twice)
W. D. Washburn Co.	president	Reorganized as Washburn Mill Company
Washburn Mill Co.	president	Became Pillsbury-Washburn, Ltd.
Pillsbury-Washburn, Ltd.	chairman	Sold to Pillsburys after receivership

Railroads and street cars

Mpls. & Duluth	president	Acquired by Mpls. & St. Louis
Mpls. & St. Louis	president	WDW replaced after sale of company
Mpls., Sault Ste. Marie & Atlantic (MSSteM&A)	president	Merged with MStP&SSteM
Mpls. & Pacific	president	Merged with MStP&SSteM
Mpls. & St. Croix	president	Merged with MStP&SSteM
Aberdeen, Bismarck & Northwestern	president	Merged with MStP&SSteM
Mpls., St. Paul & Sault Ste. Marie (Soo Line) (MStP&SSteM)	president	WDW replaced after sale to CP
1st Mpls. Street Railway	founding investor	Bankrupt in 1873 Panic
2nd Mpls. Street Railway	founding investor	Not known, no stock in estate
Peking to Hankow	founder	Never approved by Chinese government
Bismarck, Washburn & & Great Falls	president	WDW replaced after sale to Soo Line

Other businesses

Newell & Co.	partner	Sold interest
City of St. Louis	owner	Sold after one season
Minneapolis Journal	founding investor	Not known, no stock in estate
Minnesota Brush Electric	founding investor	Not known, no stock in estate
North Star Woolen Mill	owner	Not known, most likely sold
Anoka National Bank	president	Not known, no stock in estate
Anoka Opera House	owner	Burned and not replaced
Minneapolis Harvester Wks	investor, director	Sold company after ten years
Washburn Co.(foundry)	owner	Out of business
Washburn Land Co.	president	Not known, no stock in estate
Washburn Lignite Coal Co.	president	Sold after WDW's death

Real estate

Washburn Park	owner	Sold in 1908
Mpls. and Anoka properties	owner	Not known, most not in estate
Timber lands	owner	Sold as exhausted
Farms in four states	owner	Not known, not in estate

Charitable, civic, and religious

Washburn Orphan's Home	board chairman	Lifetime
Minneapolis Athenaeum	major contributor	Not known
New City Hall Commission	chairman	Disbanded after job completed
1888 Industrial Exposition	co-chairman	Disbanded after job completed
Lakewood Cemetery	founding trustee	Lifetime
First Universalist Church	founding trustee	Lifetime

Acknowledgements

Because this is the third volume I've written about the Washburn family, I feel compelled to explain why I have spent so much time on them over the past 15 years. Although I am a Washburn descendent, my interest has little to do with genealogy or family pride. In 1992, as my working career was winding down, I went back to school to pursue a long-standing love of nineteenth-century American history. My advisor at Harvard University, the late Prof. William E. Gienapp, first told me about Israel Washburn, Jr. His musing that, "nobody's ever done anything on him" redirected my life for the next eight years. I completed a thesis about Israel and earned an M.A. degree just before my seventieth birthday. Because Israel's impressive story was so little known, I rewrote it for public consumption as *Israel Washburn, Jr.—Maine's Little-Known Giant of the Civil War* (2004).

While working in Israel's papers, I became aware of his distinguished brothers and sisters. Their stories were every bit as good and as equally unknown. I wrote a number of papers about the whole tribe, and Jennifer Bunting at Tilbury House took an interest in publishing a book on the family, *Remarkable Americans, The Washburn Family* (2008).

A series of lectures across Wisconsin and Minnesota gave me further opportunities to look at documents in the Midwest and to trace the route of the original Soo Line railroad across those states. I soon realized that I had not done justice to what might be the best story of all—the rise and fall of the youngest Washburn son, William Drew.

Books, especially history books, are not written by one person alone. Since I live more than a thousand miles from where most of the events in William D. Washburn's life occurred, I relied on people and institutions across the Upper Midwest for help in assembling and verifying information. The state history libraries in Michigan, Wisconsin, Minnesota, and North Dakota were extremely helpful, especially with files of local newspapers, and with photographs.

172

The Hennepin County library system introduced me to Natalie Harte. Her help, and that of her colleague Ian Stade, was invaluable. Thanks to Natalie, I was able to scout from a distance almost 50 years' worth of newspapers and journals from Minneapolis to London. Other librarians who helped include Susan James at the Bayliss Library in Sault Ste. Marie, Ginny Hopcroft at the Bowdoin College Library, Eleanor Mills of the Perkins Library of Duke University, Susan Larson-Fleming at the Hennepin History Museum and Kathy Beauregard at the Washburn Library in Maine.

I needed a good deal of education about early railroading and milling in the Upper Midwest, which I got from people like Tim Shandel and Tom Gannon of Lake Superior Railroad Museum in Duluth, Gretchen Fossen and Gene Arduin of IXL Museum in Hermansville, and David Stevens of Mill City Museum in Minneapolis. I am indebted to Jean-Paul Viaud of Exporail Museum in Montreal for the photo of the interior of the *Saskatchewan*. The Soo Line has an active group of enthusiasts, and among those to whom I owe thanks are Stuart Nelson in Anoka, Larry Easton in Neenah, and Reid Van Sluys in Milwaukee. I'm also grateful for the time that John Terrill in Ladysmith and Pete Jensen in Escanaba gave me. Alton Chermak and David Leider in Chicago helped proof the manuscript and contributed many valuable additions and corrections. Alton found some of the more obscure small town newspaper references for me.

Descendents of both the Washburn and the Pillsbury families gave me both memories and hospitality. These generous people include AnnaBell Washburn of New York, Langhorne and Judy Washburn of Middleburg, George and Sallie Pillsbury of Wayzata, and Margaret Bergh of Minneapolis. Stan Seed of Minneapolis is not only a family member and intrepid guide, but also a genealogical bulldog. There is no Washburn gravesite that has escaped his attention—on either side of the Atlantic.

I am grateful to General Mills for their hospitality and for their wondrous company archives, recently expanded to include material from the Pillsbury Company. Sue Lappi was especially helpful in helping me find things. Brad Wallin directed me to author Dave Kenney in my quest to find out more about grain trading at the Minneapolis Exchange. I had help from four other history authors: John Driscoll housed me in Madison, John

Cooper supplied encouragement in Maine, Don Hofsommer in St. Cloud filled me in about railroading in Minnesota, and John Gjevre answered my inquiries from Moorhead. Nancy Atchison and Mikki Morrisette were among several people who helped me from the First Universalist Church. Finally, there are Tom Balcom and Bob Frame of Minneapolis, who helped unravel many mysteries, both past and present, and contributed invaluable, exhaustive, and expert third-party proofing to the manuscript's initial draft. I am also indebted to many people for the appearance of this book—mostly to Jim Peterson and the folks at DeLorme for helping me use DeLorme's fabulous mapping software to give an adequate idea of the wilderness where William built his railroads. Thanks to Al Krysan, editor Marilyn Ziebarth, and the great folks at Finney Company who helped make the final version of this book look like it does.

My thanks to everyone. There's a piece of all of you in this book.

South Freeport, Maine
May 6, 2010

Bibliography

Books

American Council of Learned Societies. *Dictionary of American Biography*. New York: Charles Scribner's Sons, 1936, 1941–45.

Arbic, Bernie, and Steinhaus, Nancy. *Upbound Downbound: The Story of the Soo Locks*. Allegan, Mich.: Priscilla Press, 2005.

Atwater, Isaac (ed.). *History of Minneapolis and Hennepin County, Minnesota*. New York: Munsell Publishing Co., 1895.

Berton, Pierre. *The Last Spike, The Great Railway, 1881–1885*. Anchor Canada (reprint), 2001.

————. *The National Dream, The Great Railway, 1871–1881*. Penguin (reprint), 1989.

Bicha, Karel D. *C. C. Washburn and the Upper Mississippi Valley*. New York: Garland Publishing, 1995.

Bohlak, Karl. *So Cold a Sky, Upper Michigan Weather Stories*. Negaunee, Mich.: Cold Sky Publishing, 2006.

Bryant, Keith L. "Railroads in the Age of Regulation, "from *Encyclopedia of American Business History and Biography*. New York: Facts on File Publications, 1988.

Castle, Henry A. (ed.). *Minnesota, Its Story and Biography*. Vol. 3. Chicago: Lewis Publishing Company, 1915.

Compendium of History and Biography of Minneapolis and Hennepin Country, Minnesota. Chicago: Henry Taylor & Company, 1914.

Congressional Record. 47 Congress, 1 sess, vol. 13, p. 2161–63. Washington, D.C.: Government Printing Office, 1882.

Donovan, Frank P. *Mileposts on the Prairie*. New York: Simmons-Boardman, 1950.

Edgar, William C. *The Medal of Gold*. Minneapolis: Bellman Co., 1925.

First Universalist Church of Minneapolis: The First 150 Years. Minneapolis: First Universalist Church of Minneapolis, 2009.

Frey, Robert L. (ed.). "Railroads in the Nineteenth Century," from *Encyclopedia of American Business History and Biography*. New York: Facts on File Publications, 1988.

Garraty, John A., and Carnes, Mark C. (eds.). *American National Biography.* New York: Oxford University Press, 1999.

Gjevre, John A. *Saga of the Soo. Vol. 3: East, West and to the North.* Moorhead, Minn.: Agassiz Publications, 2006.

Gieske, Millard L., and Keillor, Stephen J. *Norwegian Yankee, Knute Nelson and the Failure of American Politics, 1860–1923.* Northfield, Minn.: Norwegian-American Historical Association, 1995.

Goodrich, Albert M. *History of Anoka County and the Towns of Champlin and Dayton in Hennepin County, Minnesota.* Minneapolis: Hennepin Publishing Company, 1905.

Gray, James. *Business Without Boundary, The Story of General Mills.* Minneapolis: University of Minnesota Press, 1954.

Hofsommer, Don L. *Minneapolis and the Age of Railways.* Minneapolis: University of Minnesota Press, 2005.

Hofsommer, Don L. *The Tootin' Louie, A History of the Minneapolis & St. Louis Railway.* Minneapolis: University of Minnesota Press, 2005.

Holbrook, Stewart H. *James J. Hill, A Great Life in Brief.* New York: Alfred A. Knopf, 1955.

Hungerford, Edward. *Daniel Willard Rides the Line.* New York: G. P. Putnam's Sons, 1938.

Jones, Thelma. *Once Upon a Lake: A History of Lake Minnetonka and Its People.* Minneapolis: Ross and Haines, 1969.

Kane, Lucille M. *The Falls of St. Anthony, The Waterfall That Built Minneapolis.* St. Paul: Minnesota Historical Society Press, 1987.

Kenney, Dave. *The Grain Merchants, An Illustrated History of the Minneapolis Grain Exchange.* Afton, Minn.: Afton Historical Society Press, 2006.

Kinert, Reed. *Early American Steam Locomotives.* Dover Publications, 2005.

Kuhlman, Charles Byron. *The Development of the Flour-Milling Industry in the United States.* Boston: Houghton Mifflin Co., 1929.

Malone, Michael P. *James J. Hill, Empire Builder of the Northwest.* Norman: University of Oklahoma Press, 1996.

Marquis, Albert Nelson (ed.). *The Book of Minnesotans.* Chicago: A. N. Marquis and Co., 1907.

Martin, Albro. *James J. Hill and the Opening of the Northwest.* New York: Oxford University Press, 1976.

Men of Minnesota. St. Paul: R. L. Polk Co., 1915.

Minneapolis, St. Paul, and Sault Ste. Marie Railway Company. *Annual Reports,* 1888, 1889, 1900, 1902, and 1904.

Minnesota Historical Society. *Collections.* Vol. 15. St. Paul: Minnesota Historical Society, 1915.

Morgan, H. Wayne. *William McKinley and His America*. Syracuse: Syracuse University Press, 1963.

Nesbitt, Robert C. *The History of Wisconsin*. Vol. 3. Madison: State Historical Society of Wisconsin, 1985.

Poor, Henry V. *Manuals of the Railroads of the United States, 1888-1894*. New York: H.V. and H. W. Poor.

Powell, William J. *Pillsbury's Best, The Pillsbury Company*. Minneapolis: Pillsbury Co., 1985.

Railroad and Warehouse Commission of Minnesota. *Annual Reports to the Governor,* 1894 and 1895.

Ridge, Martin. *Ignatius Donnelly: The Portrait of A Politician*. Chicago: University of Chicago Press, 1962.

Shutter, Marion D. and McLain, J. S. *Progressive Men of Minnesota*. Minneapolis: Minneapolis Journal, 1897.

Sullivan, Oscar M. *The Empire Builder, A Biographical Novel of the Life of James J. Hill*. New York: Century Co., 1928.

Washburn, Edwin C. *The 17*. Englewood, New Jersey: 1929.

Washburn, Elizabeth. *The Colour of the East*. New York: Frederick A. Stokes, 1913.

Washburn, Stanley. *Nogi*. New York: Henry Holt, 1913.

Washburn, Stanley. *The Russian Advance*. Garden City: Doubleday, 1917.

Washburn, Stanley. *Trails, Trappers, and Tenderfeet in Northern Canada*. New York: Henry Holt, 1912.

Washburn, Stanley. *Victory in Defeat*. London: Constable, 1916.

Webb, Theodore A. "Washburn, A Pivotal Figure," unpublished essay, provided by author.

Wells, Henry T. *Autobiography and Reminiscences*. Minneapolis: Marshall Robinson, 1899.

White, John H., Jr. *A History of the American Locomotive— Its Development: 1830–1880*. New York: Dover Publications, 1968.

Wills, Jocelyn. *Boosters, Hustlers, and Speculators, Entrepreneurial Culture and the Rise of Minneapolis and St. Paul, 1849–1883*. St. Paul: Minnesota Historical Society Press, 2005.

Winchell, Newton H., Neill, Edward D., Williams, John F., and Bryant, Charles S. *History of the Upper Mississippi Valley*. Minneapolis: Minnesota History Co., 1881.

Journals and Newspapers

Chicago Daily Tribune
Delano Eagle
Fergus Falls Journal
Grant County Herald
London Times
Milwaukee Sentinel
Minnesota History
Minneapolis Journal
New York Press

Northwestern Miller
Sault Ste. Marie News
Soo Liner
St. Paul Daily Globe
Wahpeton Times
Wall Street Journal
Willmar Republican Gazette
Wilton News

Other

Anfinson, Scott F., "Archaeology of the Central Minneapolis Waterfront", from the *Minnesota Archaeologist Magazine*, Vol. 48, No. 1-2 1989, p20.

Angus, Fred. "The Saskatchewan," *Canadian Rail Magazine*, July–August, 1983.

A.S. Washburn papers, Duke University Library, Duke University, Durham, NC.

Baldwin, Mary Washburn. "Early Memories of Elizabeth Muzzy Washburn." Undated manuscript, Washburn Library, Livermore, Maine.

First Universalist Church of Minneapolis. Manuscript history, First Universalist Church, Minneapolis, 1909.

Frame, Robert M. "The Progressive Millers, A Cultural and Intellectual Portrait of the Flour Milling Industry, 1870–1930." Dissertation, University of Minnesota, 1980.

Frey, Martha H., "North Star Woolen Mill", *Historic American Engineering Record*, no. MN-93, pp1-12.

Gammon, Ethel (Billie). "Still No Flies on Bill?" Unpublished manuscript, in possession of Cinda Foster, Livermore, Maine.

Hunt, Gaillard. "The Life of William Drew Washburn." Undated manuscript, Washburn Library, Livermore.

Lydon, James. "History of the Soo Line." Manuscript, Minnesota Historical Society, St. Paul.

Washburn, Langhorne. Recorded conversations, 1993. Preserved by AnnaBell Washburn.

Washburn, Stanley. "Autobiography." Manuscript draft, Washburn Library, Livermore.

Index

About the Author

Photo by Martha Burns

Kerck Kelsey is a Washburn descendant and has chronicled the Washburn family for the past nineteen years. He is a historian and a story-teller who has delivered lectures on the Washburns from Maine to Alaska. Kelsey's previous books include *Israel Washburn, Jr. Maine's Little Known Giant of the Civil War*, and *Remarkable Americans: The Washburn Family*.